Issues in the Christian Initiation of Children

D1533066

Font and Table Series

General Editor: James A. Wilde

The *Font and Table Series* offers pastoral perspectives on Christian baptism, confirmation and eucharist. Other titles in the series are:

Related and available through Liturgy Training Publications

Issues in the Christian Initiation of Children
CATECHESIS AND LITURGY

Edited by Kathy Brown and Frank C. Sokol

CONTRIBUTORS

Kathy Brown

Mary Collins

Catherine Dooley

Robert D. Duggan

Linda L. Gaupin

Grace Harding

Aidan Kavanagh

Berard L. Marthaler

Richard P. Moudry

Don Neumann

Richelle Pearl-Koller

Paul J. Philibert

Frank C. Sokol

John H. Westerhoff III

LITURGY TRAINING PUBLICATIONS

Printed in the United States
Design: Jill Smith
Photography: Antonio Perez

Library of Congress Cataloging-in-Publication Data

Issues in the Christian initiation of children: catechesis and liturgy /
    edited by Kathy Brown and Frank C. Sokol; contributors, Kathy Brown...[et al.].
    Font and table series.
    Includes bibliographical references.
    ISBN 0-930467-97-3
    1. Christian education of children. 2. Initiation rites—Religious aspects—
Catholic Church. 3. Catechumens—Religious life. 4. Catholic Church—
Education—United States. I. Brown, Kathy. II. Sokol, Frank C. III. Series.
BX926.I87 1989   89-14512
264'.020812—dc20   CIP

CONTENTS

Preface

The Second Vatican Council provided rich soil for the seeds of renewal for the universal church. Catholics —adults and children—throughout the world were challenged to think anew. Commissions were established to revise the liturgical rites so that they would reflect the newly articulated ecclesiology. One such commission, responding to the mandate of the Constitution on the Sacred Liturgy to restore the catechumenate, presented to the world the *Ordo* of Christian Initiation of Adults. When decreed on January 6, 1972, few people took serious note.

Implementation was not from the top down. Rather, dedicated and adventurous men and women plunged into the new *Ordo*. They studied it, challenged it and adapted it. These people allowed it to challenge them in return about evangelization, catechesis, conversion, liturgy and more. As well, practitioners and theorists began a dialogue about Christian initiation that continues mightily today.

Many words have been written, presented, taped and published on Christian initiation, its theology, ecclesiology, christology, biblical roots, pastoral demands and practical "how to's." Exploration of the implications of Christian initiation extends to related disciplines such as adult learning, social justice, liturgy, reconciliation and catechesis. Resources, workshops, institutes and retreats developed, responding to the needs and questions of people working with the new *Ordo*.

Transformation and Restoration

A clear agenda for future dialogue has emerged regarding the initiation of children. As the catechumenate for adults continues to take root in the normal life of the church, issues and questions surface about the catechumenate for children. These questions are discussed here with some trepidation, because everyone involved with Christian initiation knows that it challenges parish practices of baptism, confirmation, eucharist and reconciliation. Being faithful to the new *Ordo* may require a transformation of current pastoral practice.

As a response to the questions raised by people involved in parish ministries of initiation, this book has a threefold purpose. First, we hope not only to respond to questions but also to raise some central questions posed by the *Ordo* for the initiation of children. Second, through these articles, we are encouraging a dialogue between practitioners and theorists. Third, we hope that this book will offer not only practical information but also a useful vision of the catechumenate as it touches all life in the church.

What Help Can We Offer?

Frank Sokol's opening chapter brings the main issues right to the front and places them in the context of the vision of the church. His answers flow directly from the text of the RCIA.

Mary Collins observes that the text of the order of Christian initiation for children, with all its rites and interstices, offers children a wonderful glimpse of God's glory and a sacramental plunge into the paschal mystery. She suggests practical ways to help children integrate the experience.

Aidan Kavanagh's discerning sketch of the catechumenate's rise and fall and his clear summary of medieval and modern reorientations elucidate the appropriate restoration of baptism, confirmation and eucharist. His grasp of the history of initiatory practice enhances his and our reflections on its contemporary implications for children.

Catherine Dooley describes the strong marriage between baptismal liturgy and baptismal catechesis during both the catechumenal and the mystagogical periods. After examining the patristic approach to catechesis in the initiatory process, she offers insightful directions for contemporary applications in the catechesis of children.

Berard Marthaler discusses the creed, doctrines, lists of doctrines and catechisms as they function in the formation of a communal faith in children. He observes that catechisms and lists of doctrines too often obscure the basic issues of the creed: the work of the Father, Son and Spirit in creation, redemption and sanctification.

Richelle Pearl-Koller reports how Christ the King Church in Minneapolis, over a period of years, went about making the initiation of children unforgettable.

Don Neumann and Kathy Brown sketch respectively the roles of peer companions and adult companions for children in the catechumenate and mystagogy. Solid relationships with peers, families and the entire community can initiate children into the whole Christ.

Linda Gaupin airs the sometimes puzzling relation of first penance, of the penitential rite (scrutiny), of conversion and of reconciliation with the sacraments of initiation for children. A specific developmental catechesis is suggested.

Grace Harding addresses the special care, language and techniques suited to children who are mentally retarded.

John Westerhoff uses several models from the behavioral sciences in examining the formation of children in the faith. He leaves no doubt that liturgical celebration is at the heart of this formation process.

Paul Philibert asks: *What* is the vehicle of ritual enculturation for children? *How* do they understand rites? *Why* are they motivated to participate in rites at all? He shows how a ritual ecology welcomes, awakens, includes, instructs, forgives, liberates, unites and empowers children.

Robert Duggan sheds light on the communal responsibility for discernment of conversion in children. In terms of covenant, Christ, the church, sacramentality, spirituality, the paschal mystery and personal transformation, Duggan outlines how discernment ought to take place in the catechumenate.

Richard Moudry challenges all of us for the future. By pointing out some of the consistencies and inconsistencies between the initiation of adults and the initiation of children in the church, he puts his finger on a core issue that must be faced. His suggestions for a pastoral strategy reflect experience and wisdom.

We want to acknowledge that two of the articles contained in this book were presented originally at the Consultation on the Catechumenate with Children sponsored by the North American Forum on the Catechumenate in December of 1988. The presentations of Mary Collins and Paul J. Philibert were subsequently published in the March 1989 issue of *Catechumenate: A Journal of Christian Initiation*. We thank the authors, Forum and *Catechumenate* for permission to reprint the articles here.

We thank those who have given of their time and energy in reading and typing the manuscripts included in this book, especially Pat Mullen, Barbara Mattus and Janet Towner.

It is our hope that this book will contribute to the success of the ministry of the many people who are courageously attempting to implement the *Ordo* of Christian initiation with children while still remaining faithful to its vision.

— *Kathy Brown*
— *Frank C. Sokol*

CHAPTER
1

> "The catechumenate with children involves attitudinal changes on the part of both children and adults that allow us to respect them because they are children, not because they will someday be adults."

The Catechumenate for Children of Catechetical Age: What, Who, How, Why?

FRANK C. SOKOL

The Rite of Christian Initiation of Adults (RCIA) has been discovered as the crown of the sacramental revisions of the Second Vatican Council. In much the same way the chapter within the RCIA concerning the initiation of children is being discovered as a major gem in that crown. Even though it is largely unpolished at this time, the catechumenate with children has the potential of reflecting the best of the church's tradition and of refining the church's initiation policies for the future.

As this chapter of the RCIA is studied and implemented by theorists and practitioners, many questions are raised. The experience of increasing numbers of children of catechetical age seeking initiation in the church causes pastoral ministers to look for structures that are faithful to general principles of the catechumenate and at the same time are sensitive to the circumstances of children.

Our discussion seeks to raise the most basic questions and to respond according to the church's vision of a consistent initiation practice. The responses are not yet complete; they only mine the gem. Further study and practice are needed to polish the catechumenate with children and set it in the crown of the RCIA.

What Is It?

The catechumenate for children of catechetical age is the order by which children become members of the church. It is a part of a larger repertory of rituals contained in the RCIA, which guides the church in receiving new members. The RCIA was approved for use by Pope Paul VI in January, 1972, translated into English in 1974 and, with some additions and revisions, mandated by the United States bishops in September, 1988. The catechumenate for children of catechetical age is the normal and official way of forming children in the faith of the church and celebrating their conversion through the sacraments of baptism, confirmation and eucharist.

It is significant that, in the edition of the International Commission on English in the Liturgy used by our National Conference of Catholic Bishops, this section on the initiation of children appears in the church's ritual texts as chapter 1 of part 2 of the RCIA. The section for children is part of the inclusive vision of Christian formation for all church members. An enlightened way to begin the catechumenate for children is to read, study and experience the catechumenate for adults. The catechumenate principles that govern the adult rite are the norms for adapting the process to other groups, children among them. From this perspective, the initiation of children is connected intimately to the ongoing conversion of the adult community.

In the catechumenate there is a progression of three major rites, each with periods of preparation and follow-up. These four periods, which lead to and flow from the rites, are times of formation. They include experiences of what the church believes and lives and how the church prays and serves. This structure offers room for much adaptation. Fidelity to the general principles of the catechumenate enables greater fidelity to its structure.

For Whom Is the Rite?

The "catechumenate for children of catechetical age" is a phrase that carries multiple interpretations. A clarification is attempted in RCIA, 252: It is for children not baptized as infants; children who have attained the use of reason and are of catechetical age; children presented by their parents or guardians or who present themselves with parental permission; children capable of receiving a personal faith and recognizing an obligation of conscience; children dependent on their parents or guardians and influenced by their companions.

Children who enter the catechumenate could be sons or daughters of catechumens or church members who are returning to active participation. In some instances they are children whose parents belong to other churches or to no church.

Most commentators interpret "catechetical age" to include children between ages 7 to 17. By the age of 7 children usually begin their more formal religious formation (and their more formal general education). By the age of 18, persons seeking initiation are placed more properly with adults.

How Does It Work?

A basic premise of the catechumenate is that the rites celebrate the journey of conversion. The focal points of the process are these rites because they evolve from a period of formation and at the same time they anticipate the formation in the period to follow. Obviously liturgy is not all that happens during the catechumenate. But liturgy unites the entire journey and articulates ritually the formation taking place in the catechumens and in the Christian community. To describe how the catechumenate works involves looking first at the rites to determine what is being celebrated. Then it will be easier to mark a path for the periods that precede and follow each rite.

The First Major Rite. Acceptance into the Order of Catechumens presumes an initial awakening of faith and a basic belief in Jesus Christ. The rite itself calls for the children to express their desire to join the Christian family and to come to a deeper knowledge of Jesus Christ. The children are presented with two primary symbols of the Christian community, the cross and the Bible, as guides for their journey into an ever deeper faith.

Based on this rite, the period of inquiry that precedes it is for awakening faith. It is a time for the children and community members to get acquainted and an opportunity for children to ask their most basic questions. The period of inquiry can help children learn what it means to be "Christlike" when catechists offer stories of other Christians as models. A healthy environment for relational experiences is important so that these Christian stories may be linked to the stories lived in the families and communities of these children.

For children of catechetical age an ensemble of settings is helpful for this initial awakening of faith. Along with the most natural setting of their homes, they now are creating other comfortable environments with peers, whom the text of the RCIA refers to as their "companions." The catechumenate team may capitalize on this desire to be part of a group of companions as a logical setting for the development of faith. A third locale is the special sessions where the catechumens gather together with their sponsors to discuss specific issues of their life of faith. These three settings—home, catechesis with peers (religious education programs or school) and catechumenal sessions with adults—work together to cultivate the initial stirrings of faith. Acceptance into the Order of Catechumens functions as a door leading from the initial stirring of faith to an experience of the Christian community that nourishes the growth of that faith.

The Second Major Rite. Election or Enrollment of Names presumes that a deepening of faith has occurred and that the catechumens can identify themselves as followers of Jesus Christ. Before the bishop accepts the names of the catechumens for enrollment, he asks their parents and godparents four questions: Are they sincere in their desire? Have they listened to the word? Have they tried to live as his faithful followers? Have they joined the community in prayer and service? This is what occurs during the period of the catechumenate, which precedes the rite of election.

The description of this period that is outlined in RCIA, 75, remains the same when applied to children of catechetical age. Considered by some to be one of the most significant statements, RCIA, 75, explains that the deepening of faith during the catechumenate has several dimensions: formation in the church's teachings, formation in the life of the Christian community, formation in the prayer of the church and formation in service to the world.

Because the scriptures are the central text for catechesis, it is important to develop in children a sense of attentive listening. The Bible presented to them earlier should be reverenced and used. In the catechumenate, as in the period of inquiry, the three basic environments of home, peer catechesis and special catechumenal sessions with adults are all significant for the deepening of faith.

The Third Major Celebration: Initiatory Sacraments. The sacraments of initiation presume a refinement of the faith of the children and the development of a sense of belonging to the community of faith. During the initiatory rite of baptism the presider leads the children, and subsequently their godparents and the assembly, in a renunciation of sin and a profession of faith. While the entire Easter Vigil, which is the appropriate time for the celebration of initiation, is filled with the vibrant symbols of the faith, this renunciation and profession can be the focus of the preceding period. Then follow the initiatory rites of chrismation and eucharist.

The formation time before the sacraments of initiation is concurrent with the season of Lent and is called the period of purification and enlightenment. It is a time *to be* precisely what *God invites one to become:* purified and enlightened. The promises made by the elect before baptism are the result of this time of spiritual discovery. The twofold structure of the baptismal promises—renunciation and profession—indicates a basic and profound movement for children: turning away from what is bad and turning toward what is good. Baptismal promises

7

are not simply answers to questions or the recitation of the creed. They are a way of believing and a way for living.

A significant help to children for purification and enlightenment is to uncover with them the presence of God already in their lives. The baptized community of faith can be a catalyst for naming the innate sense of the transcendent that children possess. By helping to disclose God's presence and action in all things for children, it becomes easier to discern with them the "bad" things to be avoided and the "good" things to be achieved.

Before the celebration of the initiatory rites, the time of personal purification and enlightenment, as well as enculturation with the community, takes place at home, in peer catechetical settings and in special catechumenal sessions with adults, along with the evangelical scrutinies and exorcisms, presentations, anointings and celebrations of the word.

After the celebration of the initiatory rites, the Sunday eucharist affords opportunities for an abiding development of faith and lasting reflection on that faith. This period after initiation is called mystagogy, a celebrative time for allowing the sacramental newness to resonate or echo throughout the child's thinking and behavior.

Following their initiation, the children should maintain prominent positions within the liturgical assembly. Throughout the Easter season, the status of the neophytes should be reflected in their places among the celebrating assembly. Their manner of listening to the word of God can even be an example to fellow Christians. Among the baptized they enjoy "pride of place."

Mystagogy also offers more systematic reflection on the mysteries of God's grace, made visible and tangible in the initiatory sacraments. This is a time for sacramental cate-chesis—a time for understanding more deeply and living more fully the mysteries celebrated in initiation.

The integration of the fully initiated children into the community is a significant dimension of mystagogy. At the same time the mediation of God's presence through their companions should be respected also. Neophytes need to gather regularly with these companions to receive support and to experience the riches of sharing faith.

By maintaining Sunday eucharist as the primary setting for mystagogy and keeping the gatherings of family, peer catechesis and sessions with adults, the new young Christians continue to celebrate their faith in God and their service to the wider world.

Our discussion on how the catechumenate with children works is based on a simple premise: The rites of the order of initiation set the agenda for leading children through the conversion journey. Fidelity to the rites is the guide for what happens in the periods of the catechumenate.

Why Use This Order for Children?

The order of Christian initiation for children of catechetical age is a valuable gift not only for the end (a sacramental celebration) but also for the journey (a sacramental life). The catechumenate with children involves attitudinal changes on the part of both children and adults that allow us to respect them *because* they are children, not because they will someday be adults. People who minister in the catechumenate with children of catechetical age grow in their respect for the dignity of being a child and the unique ways that a child communicates with others and with the Other. Yes, the community ministers to children, but children also minister to the community. When the plurality of ministries is listed for the catechumenate with children, it is wise to list first the ministry of the children.

The what, who, how and why of the catechumenate for children leads to this simple conclusion: Welcoming children into the community of faith and forming them in its life continues to raise new, good questions for each generation of Christians. As long as the correct questions are being asked, the correct answers always can be found.

CHAPTER 2

"*For the child, the word of grace is a powerful, if mysterious, presence. For the child, giving some real shape to the interior life and coming to terms with the outer world, matching inner and outer worlds, is infinitely fascinating. Shaping and coming to terms are human tasks; they happen only in relationships.*"

Order for the Christian Initiation of Children: The Ritual Text

MARY COLLINS

R ituals are about relationships. Religious rituals celebrate redemptive relationships. The liturgical order for the Christian initiation of children mediates a whole series of redemptive relationships that give shape to a child's identity as a social and religious person. The task is to reflect and expand on the official liturgical text that provides the context for the Christian initiation of children. We will not go through it line by line, numbered section by numbered section. Rather we will reflect on two matters that meet in these pages: the child's life situation and the church's religious understanding of the mystery into which children are being initiated.

Life Situation of the Child

Cognitive, moral, social and religious development in children have been the stuff of much solid research in our day. I do not pretend to be an expert in such matters, nor even a careful and experienced observer of ordinary children on a day-to-day basis. I take my testimony from literature that rings of truth. Pulitzer prize author Annie Dillard's 1987 autobiography, *An American*

Childhood, and Flannery O'Connor's short story, "A Temple of the Holy Ghost," will provide some common images for remembering the child's experience of relating to the world and to the mystery of God.

Dillard recounts for us the uncovering of her interior life and her discovery of the exterior world from ages 5 through 17. At the surface level, the book is a secular journal, and one of its final chapters begins "I quit the church," a statement that makes it of dubious value for a consultation concerned with young people coming to the church. But nothing Annie Dillard writes is "merely secular," as the book's epigraph reveals: "I have loved, O Lord, the beauty of thy house and the place where dwelleth thy glory" (Psalm 26).

The metaphor Dillard uses for coming to see the beauty and the glory, the mystery of God, the uncovering of her interior life is "waking up."

> Children 10 years old wake up, and find themselves here, discover themselves to have been here all along. . . . They wake, like sleepwalkers, in full stride; they wake like people brought back from cardiac arrest or from drowning: *in medias res,* surrounded by familiar people and objects, equipped with a hundred skills. They know the neighborhood, can read and write English . . . and yet they feel themselves to have just stepped off the boat, just converged with their bodies, just flown down from a trance, to lodge in an eerily familiar life already under way.

Of herself, Annie Dillard says,

> I woke in bits, like all children, piecemeal over the years. I discovered myself and the world, and forgot them, and discovered them again. I woke at intervals until [by my tenth summer] the intervals of waking tipped the scales, and I was more often aware than not. I noticed this process of waking, and predicted with terrifying logic that one of these years not far away I would be awake continuously and never slip back, and never be free of myself again.

Ten is a time for waking up in wonderful ways to what is going on inside and outside oneself. At 10, says Annie Dillard, "The great outer world hove into view and began to fill with things that had apparently been there all along: mineralogy, detective work, lepidopterology, ponds and streams, flying, society." Many children of the 1980s have less benign outer worlds than the one Annie Dillard knew in Pittsburgh in the 1950s. But it is the child's task to enter into relationship with—to come to terms with—what is all around.

The child's interior awakening is another kind of challenge. "The interior life is often stupid," she writes. "Its egoism blinds it and deafens it; its imagination spins out ignorant tales, fascinated. . . . A mind risks real ignorance for the sometimes paltry prize of an imagination enriched." She makes her observations about playing childhood illusion against known reality in the context of recalling a common childhood experience: seeing lights travel across a darkened bedroom wall without being able at first to tell where the light comes from—and then entertaining again and again a terror even after finding out that the light racing over the wall is nothing more than the headlights of a passing car. "The interior life is often stupid. . . . The trick of *reason* is to get the imagination to seize the actual world—if only from time to time." Children want to know what is real and what is illusion. But it takes practice and help to bring the interior life into contact with the real.

Catechists regularly work with children who are waking up to the world, to life, to themselves, to God. "Children of catechetical age" is what the order for the Christian initiation of children calls them. Catechists have accepted responsibility for bringing the message of the gospel to such children's attention as the most real of the stuff they are encountering. What is at once both challenging and sobering is the realization that these children, waking up piecemeal and discovering they are in a world already spinning, are hungry for the word of grace.

Dillard says of herself and her summer Bible camp experiences, "I had a head for religious ideas. They were the first ideas I ever encountered. They made other ideas seem mean."

She recalls, "I had miles of Bible in my memory. . . . There was no corner of my brain where you couldn't find, among the files of clothing labels and heaps of rocks, among the swarms of protozoans and shelves of novels, whole tapes and snarls and reels of Bibles." She quotes from childhood memory:

James and John, the sons of Zebedee, he made them fishers of men. And he came to the Lake of Gennesaret, and he came to Capernaum. And he withdrew in a boat. And a certain man went down from Jerusalem to Jericho. See it here on the map? Down. He went down, and fell among thieves.

And the swine jumped over the cliff.

And the voice cried, Samuel, Samuel. And the wakened boy Samuel answered, Here am I. And at last he said, Speak.

Hear, O Israel, the Lord is one.

And Peter said, I know him not; I know him not; I know him not. And the rich young ruler said, What must I do? And the woman wiped his feet with her hair. And he said, Who touched me?

And he said, Verily, verily, verily, verily; life is not a dream. Let this cup pass from me. If it be thy will, of course, only if it be thy will.

For the child, the word of grace is a powerful, if mysterious, presence. For the child, giving some real shape to the interior life and coming to terms with the outer world, matching inner and outer worlds, is infinitely fascinating. Shaping and coming to terms are human tasks; they happen only in relationships. And rituals, too, are about relationships. So let us turn our attention to the liturgical order for the Christian initiation of children. The church prepared this order for itself in 1972 as a way to help children shape their interior lives and to come to terms with the world around them. The church offers it as a structure for celebrating the redemptive relationships at the heart of a child's life. It offers us a language of words and gestures and interactions that we can in turn offer to children to help them name what is real and valuable.

The Order: Some Preliminary Observations

First, we are dealing with a liturgical order, a series of rites and periods that, taken together, celebrate and resonate the one mystery of our salvation in Christ. An unfortunate early English translation from the Latin labeled the liturgical order for Christian initiation *(Ordo initiationis christianae adultorum)* a "rite"—and so the acronym RCIA. Now the name is stuck.

Nevertheless, I am going to use the term "order" to name the whole process envisioned and to reserve the word "rite" to designate the specific liturgical celebrations that structure the movement through the process of Christian initiation of children.

Second, the order for the Christian initiation of children is a subsection ("Christian Initiation of Children Who Have Reached Catechetical Age") within a larger liturgical order, the *Order for the Christian Initiation of Adults*. The order for children is a variant, not a separate order. It appears as a chapter within the adult order, adjusting the adult order to the perceived special needs of school-age children. It is imperative that we keep this larger initiatory order in mind. One cannot comprehend the vision or intent of the Rite of Christian Initiation for Adults (RCIA, 252–330), the paragraphs focused on the initiation of children, unless one reads the section and interprets it in the context of RCIA, 1–251, the rites for adults. The children, waking up to an inner life and an outer world, are to be initiated into the faith according to the most ancient Christian pattern, recently restored, of a liturgical catechumenate. The decision to bring children to mindfulness in this way was not made lightly. It was made knowingly. The decision was made knowing that it introduces pastoral tension into our parishes and dioceses.

The decision was made knowing that most Catholic children in the United States are still being baptized as infants, confessed and communicated at age 7 and confirmed somewhere between ages 12 and 18. Catechists know this. The National Conference of Catholic Bishops knew this when they acted to promulgate this order in every United States diocese. Pastors, pastoral workers and parents are still learning existentially that these two pastoral programs for children's initiation into the sacramental life of the church diverge. The divergence of the programs means some decisions lie ahead for the bishops: How will they reconcile the differences? Will they dare in our lifetime to baptize, confirm and communicate those who are presented as infants and to think about appropriate lifelong Christian formation for those who come to the Easter sacraments shortly after birth?

We can only guess what bishops will do in the future about these pastoral tensions. But do not let yourselves be seduced or confused or compromised by or lose your nerve in the face of the inconsistency of the present pastoral situation. Your task is to implement the order for the Christian initiation of children, an order that embraces the vision of the adult order, the ancient pattern newly restored, marked by the moments of reception as catechumen and catechesis, election and scrutiny, the Easter sacraments and mystagogy.

Third, be alert to the pastoral reality that the promulgation of a liturgical order is inevitably followed by a process of *reception,* the process by which the liturgical order is actually appropriated and used within the churches. We have almost 20 years' experience in using the *Ordo Missae.* We are less experienced with the new order for Christian initiation; we are least experienced of all with this chapter on the initiation of school-age children. You will be giving shape to the reception of this order in the United States by the very way you work with this text. Recognize that the text does not answer all your questions. Nor is there a single right way to interpret a directive, even though the context for correct interpretation is clear: the adult order. Some things you will have to discover as you go forward, reflecting with the children and their families. There is room for imaginative use of the texts; there is no authorization for disregarding the order merely because it will make new demands on all of us as a church. Learn from your experiences; listen to what others have learned; keep the good. Above all else, keep your focus on the spiritual awakening of the children, not on what is comfortable and familiar for adults and so will take least effort and adjustment for them.

Relationships of Salvation

Who are these children whose relationships with the living God, with the fragile human community, with the wounded cosmos, we hope to shape as the church of Jesus Christ? Who are these children whom the living God touches through us? The order itself is vague: These are "school-age children," not yet adults, dependent on their parents but moving out into the larger world, with their already baptized peers as companions. That composite profile says to me that we could be talking about children as young as 6 or 7 and as old as 20 or 21. Most of the interpretative literature presumes the children are 7 to 12, preadolescent. But some of you must be facing the challenge of dealing with the Christian initiation of adolescents from 13 to 18.

I invite you to become present imaginatively to your own local collection of preadolescent and adolescent boys and girls. Keep them in mind as we focus first not on the ritual moments of the order—the rite of reception as a catechumen, the rite of election and scrutiny, and the Easter sacraments—but on the interstices between those ritual moments. (Dictionary: For "interstices" I found as a third usage the notation, "Roman Catholic, the intervals of time required by canon law before promotion to a higher level of ordination." Our usage is a fourth, by analogy: the periods intervening between the ritual moments in Christian initiation.) Our interest in the interstices of the initiation process is not simply on the fact of time elapsing, but on what happens with the children before the liturgical rite of reception into the catechumenate, what happens with the children in the months and even years before the church names them among the elect, what the church understands itself to be doing when it brings their young lives to scrutiny in the light of the gospel and what plans we as church are making to accompany them in the long Christian formation through their remaining years of childhood and adolescence. Frankly, it will be a lot easier to focus energies on the liturgical celebrations that punctuate the process of initiation than to face the troublesome question: What do we do to present Jesus Christ as good news to these children?

At one level, it is important to try to understand the text as a text. Who are the sponsors? Who are the godparents? Who are the companions? What are they supposed to be doing? When do these children meet together in their identity as catechumens?

When do they meet with all the children of the church? Why did the Roman *Ordo* omit a liturgical rite of election for children? Why does the United States adaptation make it optional? What is the difference between a scrutiny and a penitential rite? What is the purpose of putting together in a single liturgical celebration the first confession of the children baptized as infants and the evangelical scrutiny of the young catechumens? Are we free not to do it? The list of questions is long; many of them have already been treated in published articles.

But as I read the literature I have a strong hunch that we really don't know yet how we want to answer those questions. We can answer them speculatively; we can try to fathom the minds of the liturgiologists who prepared the texts. In doing so, we may learn *their* hypothetical answers. But existential answers will come from vital churches who develop lively processes of catechesis, enlightenment and mystagogy for the interstices between the liturgical events.

The text as it comes to us has problems. To single out one: I have a hard time imagining from a liturgical or theological viewpoint how to celebrate in a single ritual event first confessions of 7-year-olds and the evangelical scrutiny of young catechumens (see RCIA, 293). I have a hard time because these are different liturgical events that belong to two different orders of Christian initiation operating side by side in our church, and I would not be disposed to mix them. I do not think it is sound theologically or pastorally, even though the rite suggests it and familiarity with both children's confessions and penance celebrations will make it seem reasonable.

Does that mean I find no place for bringing together the young catechumens and their baptized peers, some of whom are anticipating confession and communion, some of whom are anticipating confirmation, some of whom are in a period of continuing Christian formation for the young? On the contrary, their associations can be mutually beneficial. But what form these faith-sharing and community-building meetings take should correspond to natural rhythms in the social lives of children and to their human capacities for religious development. Until we look at the composition of a specific catechumenal group, we are not in a position to make a judgment about a suitable program for peer companionship in the journey of faith.

Rather than giving abstract or speculative answers to questions posed by the text of the order for the Christian initiation of children, we need to remember what we are about by returning to key paragraphs of the order of Christian initiation of adults. Among these we might choose RCIA, 1 or 4. In RCIA, 1, we read that this whole liturgical order is designated for those adults—and by analogy, for those children of catechetical age—"who, after hearing the mystery of Christ proclaimed, consciously and freely seek the living God and enter the way of faith and conversion as the Holy Spirit enters their hearts."

This is the person "who consciously and freely seeks the living God" after "hearing the mystery of Christ proclaimed." Can this description of the adult candidate also describe the 7-to-10-year-old child "waking up piecemeal" to life itself? The description at least reminds us that we as church are preparing the children above all else to embrace a relationship with the living God. We prepare them by telling them the story of Jesus, because it is in that story, so we believe, that the living God is revealed. That story assures them in a suffering world that they can trust the mystery and risk being touched by the holiness of God. But how shall we tell them the story of Jesus? Certainly it is a story of God's love, yet we tell it truthfully only if we recall Dorothy Day's observation that love in storybooks may be sweet and comforting, but love in practice is a harsh and dreadful thing.

Paragraph 4 of the RCIA states that adult catechumens—and so by analogy, preadolescent catechumens—are to be brought to reflect on "the value of the paschal mystery." What an interesting phrase: "the value of the paschal mystery," that harsh and dreadful but powerfully real redemptive love of God! In our consumer, materialist, utilitarian, free-enterprise culture —the dominant culture in which we are socializing our children

—something that is valuable is useful. It pays off. It's worth the effort, worth the time. It's good for something, not simply good in itself. Nevertheless, the text suggests that "the value of the paschal mystery" is worthy of reflection even by the young.

This is where the children's catechumenate gets hard for the adult church, for children have an uncanny way of spotting discrepancies in adult lives. Annie Dillard remembered her discovery of adult inconsistency in this way:

> Why did they spread this scandalous document [the Bible] before our eyes? If they had read it, I thought, they would have hid it. They didn't recognize the vivid danger that we would, through repeated exposure, catch a case of its wild opposition to their world. Instead they bade us study great chunks of it, and think about those chunks, and commit them to memory and ignore them.

Children whose vision is not yet clouded over by the cataracts of the dominant culture's values can see uncommon value even in the outrageous claims the gospel makes about the worth of the paschal mystery. Flannery O'Connor, like Annie Dillard, has been able to hold onto and find language for the child's awe of divine holiness whose presence is recognized even in life's most absurd situations. O'Connor's short story, "The Temple of the Holy Ghost," recounts the inner musings of a child who overhears her older cousins giggling at Sister's insistence to the girls that their bodies are temples of the Holy Ghost. These same giggling cousins move on to other shocking topics, among them, seeing a sideshow freak in a traveling circus, a person who was "both a man and a woman," who nevertheless kept praising God with evangelical fervor.

The child found it plausible, not at all funny, as she mused on and tangled these uncommon possibilities in her mind when she was drifting off to sleep: her own body, the sideshow wonder, her stupid cousins, the moon-faced nun, the neighbor boy with ears shaped like a pig's—all made according to the design of the living God, all temples of the Holy Ghost. For the child, the "paschal mystery" of human brokenness transfigured by glory was indeed a revelation, but not an implausible one.

Adolescents more likely find the value of the paschal mystery less plausible, reason for disbelief and even scorn. Only rarely do they possess the contemplative vision that sees wholeness and the holiness of God showing through life's absurdities. So the stupid cousins giggle, and Annie Dillard left the church for a while at age 16. As she explained the problem to her pastor, why all this suffering if the all-powerful Creator directs the world? She had studied the problem: the Book of Job and C. S. Lewis:

> Addressing this question, I found 30 pages written thousands of years ago, and 40 pages written in 1955. They offered a choice of fancy language saying, "Forget it," or serenely worded, logical-sounding answers that so strained credibility (pain is God's megaphone) that "Forget it" seemed in comparison a fine answer.

Celebrating the reception of children in the order of catechumens can be a splendid liturgical event. But if it is to be a celebration in spirit and in truth, the adult community will have to become newly pensive about "the value of the paschal mystery" about which they intend to catechize the young. While younger children's ability to wonder at the beauty and the glory of God's world and to anticipate their own joyful sacramental plunge into the paschal mystery may well renew the Christian joy of the adults who support them, the disbelief of the adolescent catechumens may have the power to bring their adult sponsors to humility in the face of their own unbelief, and so to silence and to prayer. Yes, the catechumenal presentation of the mystery of the living God must correspond to the children's spiritual capacity. And yes, it is our primary purpose in gathering children into the catechumenate that they and we might seek the living God, not the god of our illusions or an idol of our own cultural making.

When this spiritual journey is begun in faith and with confidence in the living God, then such acts as signing foreheads and ears and hands with the cross, presenting gospel books, anointing with oils for strengthening, enrolling names, proclaiming creeds, asking adults to give witness by their own lives and to testify to grace at work in the lives of the children— all these will become more and more the simple acts and familiar gestures of the household of the faith. Because we have become increasingly adept at staging liturgical events in this past decade, parishes will figure out how to "do" the rites for the Christian initiation of children. What we need now is to give our liturgical celebrations "heart," the fruit of our own struggles with the living God revealed in the paschal mystery.

Evangelical Scrutiny of the Young

Earlier I had used the phrase "evangelical scrutiny of young catechumens" to talk about what the liturgical order names the "penitential rite." I want to return here to a more extensive reflection on the theological and liturgical problems enmeshed in this hybrid rite. I made a decision to do my own naming of the ritual event because of my dissatisfaction with the text's name and with the dangerous confusion it introduces in paragraph 295. My naming captures better, I think, the spirit of paragraph 139 of the Order of Christian Initiation of Adults, the norm from which this children's rite is adapted.

In paragraph 139 we read of the final stage of the initiation process, which begins with the rite of election:

> This is a period of more intense spiritual preparation, consisting more in interior reflection than in catechetical instruction, and is intended to purify the minds and hearts of the elect as they search their own consciences and do penance. The period is intended as well to enlighten the minds and hearts of the elect with a deeper knowledge of Christ the Savior.

If that is what the period is about—"intense spiritual preparation" and "deeper knowledge of Christ the Savior"— then that is what the liturgical event designated for this period should be celebrating.

My term, "evangelical scrutiny," may not yet be the final word for naming the liturgical event celebrated within the time of purification and enlightenment. But it does serve to remind us that the focus must continue to be on God's gracious judgment of these children, God's embrace of their and our broken and wounded humankind. Socially, the children may be wretches, at times deceitful, violent, abusive of others, aggressive, malicious, manipulative. After all, they are our children, and it is as the children of earth that they have been chosen to hear the good news of God's redeeming love.

Catholic catechesis for conscience formation, guided by a Jansenist moralism and Irish-American guilt as a clerical cultural style, has regularly been derailed from the path of the gospel. We have been more fascinated with human evil and human depravity than with God's mercy. We have found it easier to teach self-loathing than to wonder together at the mystery of God's love for us as unlikely "temples of the Holy Ghost." "Evangelical scrutiny" is my way of holding my own attention, and directing yours, to the true center of gravity for this liturgy and the reflection that leads up to it.

Unfortunately, the liturgical rite presented in the text for the Christian initiation of children encourages that chronic Catholic drift from the center that is Christ to fascination with our own sinful acts and corrupt natures. Say "penitential rite" to adult Catholics—the catechists, parents, liturgists, pastors—and our emotional warehouses begin delivering guilt at the loading dock. Lists of sins tick out in the front offices as the bills of lading. How apt is the text (RCIA, 295) when it says that the "penitential rite" offered there will have different meanings for different participants. Stretch what I think should be a genuine evangelical scrutiny of the young catechumens into an occasion where first communicants, parents, godparents and sponsors all also go to confession, and the emotional rockets of the adults in most assemblies will dim the light of Christ in their glare! They will also block our ability to see the cosmic "sin of the world," so caught up do we get in our own tawdriness.

The whole church needs to have its life brought into evangelical scrutiny if we are going to get our broken lives into clearer paschal perspective. The order of Christian initiation of children, with its period of enlightenment evangelically conceived and its penitential rite well celebrated, has the potential to begin this much-needed reorientation. We must begin to celebrate well this mystery of our deliverance from the sin of the world and our reconciliation by God's graciousness. We cannot risk losing this new opportunity for public evangelical scrutiny of the church by treating it as something familiar, as ho-hum as confession.

A model for authentic evangelical scrutiny is found in Luke 19: in Zacchaeus, fascinated with Jesus, and Jesus, openly welcoming and spending some time with an unenlightened Zacchaeus. As the scripture reports the encounter, it is only after sustained association with Jesus and reflection on the meeting that this unenlightened man began to see his own life differently. Zacchaeus began to change his behavior, seeing himself only as reprobate in the light of Jesus. Jesus' judgment on the event is recorded, "Today salvation has come to this house." Remembering Zacchaeus, we must so celebrate the evangelical scrutiny that all who assemble are able to see immediately, or on reflection, the goodness of God in all its brilliance. Such light can enlighten us for our lifetimes.

Unfortunately, the wording of the prayer texts for the scrutiny of children of catechetical age is tilted to trigger guilt rather than enlightenment. How evangelically enlightening is the proposed dialogue of paragraph 300?

> Celebrant: Even though they try to live as your children, they sometimes find this difficult.
>
> Children: Father, we want always to do what pleases you, but sometimes we find this hard.

The voice we hear is not the voice of Christ proclaiming salvation from cosmic evil. We hear rather the annoyed adult whose pleasure or peace has been frustrated by disruptive children's behavior.

How much better the audacious dialogue of the sideshow freak imagined by the child as a liturgical response to the burden of brokenness and sin taken up in the mystery of Christ!

> "God has made me thisaway and I don't dispute it,"
>   and the people saying, "Amen, Amen."
> "You! You are God's temple, don't you know? don't you know?
>   God's Spirit has a dwelling in you, don't you know?"
>   "Amen, Amen."
> "A temple of God is a holy thing."
>   "Amen, Amen."

"I am a temple of the Holy Ghost."
"Amen."

The people began to slap their hands without making a loud noise and with a regular beat between the Amens, more and more softly, as if they knew there was a child near, half asleep.

When our young catechumens hear and wonder that this good news might really be true, when they see that the wounded adult church nevertheless witnesses as best it can to the truth of salvation in Jesus, the children will be ready to be brought to the font and to the table, enlightened by evangelical scrutiny. The subsequent period of mystagogy, followed by Christian formation through adolescence to adulthood, will afford many occasions for them to reflect on behavior worthy of "temples of the Holy Ghost." As the adult Zacchaeus, when he came to know Jesus, decided to share his belongings with the poor and to make restitution to those he had defrauded, the children will learn from their sustained association with the body of Christ, the deeds of justice and integrity and how to walk in the path of righteousness. When they see adults ready to repent and to confess behavior incompatible with their identity as temples surrounded everywhere by other temples, then the children will be ready for the sacrament of reconciliation, celebrated now from the viewpoint of evangelical enlightenment.

Summary

Three statements summarize my reflections on this text. First, the initiation of children through the liturgical catechumenate is to be understood as a variant of the larger liturgical order for the Christian initiation of adults. Second, the theological vision of the whole order is to bring the children to see the value of the paschal mystery. Third, the liturgical rites with their accompanying catechesis, enlightenment and mystagogical reflection are the way the church initiates children as well as adults into redemptive relationship with the living God, with the church summoned by the power of the Holy Spirit in the name of Jesus and with the whole created world. If we lose sight of these matters, there is no reason to direct the limited energies and resources of parishes and dioceses toward the development of one more unassimilated postconciliar liturgical project, a catechumenate for children.

CHAPTER

3

"*The church has always baptized infants and will always do so. Catholic instinct finds it inconceivable that John the Baptist placed age restrictions on those he baptized, that Jesus did not embrace children or use them as images of faith.*"

Initiating Children: Historical Sketch and Contemporary Reflections

AIDAN KAVANAGH

The church has always baptized infants and will always do so. Catholic instinct finds it inconceivable that John the Baptist placed age restrictions on those he baptized; that Jesus did not embrace children or use them as images of faith (Matthew 18:1–6; Mark 9:33–37; 10:13–16; Luke 9:46–48; 18:15–17); that the apostles baptized entire pagan households except their infants and young children (Acts 2:37–39). Nor is there the slightest evidence in liturgical history that there was ever a time when the liturgy of Christian baptism excluded infants or young children. Indeed, faithful to the Lord's own teaching, the liturgy has both embraced children and held them up as paradigms of faith for all age groups coming to baptism: "So put away all malice and all guile and insincerity and envy and all slander. Like newborn babes, long for the spiritual milk, that by it you may grow up to salvation, for you have tasted the kindness of the Lord" (1 Peter 2:1–3). Salvation in Christ knows no exclusions by age.

33

The Rise and Fall of the Catechumenate

Facts such as the foregoing, however, are never inert. They are always deployed, often differently from era to era and according to fluctuations in cultural outlook, pastoral necessity, theology and sentiment. On the whole, the history of the decline in numbers of adult converts and the consequent fading of the catechumenate is the history of the rise in numbers of infant baptisms. It is also the history of the Christianization of the various cultures of North Africa, the Middle East, Europe and later Russia, a remarkable achievement by a religious movement that was legally illicit until the early 300s and still remained a cognitive minority in many places for another two or three centuries. Except in Armenia and Ethiopia, it largely failed east of Mesopotamia and south of Palestine. But its successes inevitably redeployed the facts of its evangelical and initiatory foundations, causing them to be sensed in different ways.

One such way was, understandably, a spreading presumption, supported by practice, that the normal way of becoming a Christian was by baptism in infancy; baptizing adults, although not unknown, was increasingly exceptional. One can see this shift in the gradual atrophying of the catechumenal structure in the Roman liturgical system itself. From a detailed three-year catechumenate in Hippolytus's *Apostolic Tradition* (c. 215–20), it seems that by the seventh century the catechumenate had become mostly a formality and the candidates for baptism mostly infants: The great lenten scrutinies of catechumens were moved from Sundays to weekdays; the baptizands were carried *(deportantur)* and were to be kept from nursing at the breast *(ablactantur)* before receiving first communion after their baptism and confirmation.[1] And while the Roman system kept on its official books its ancient single rite of initiation, meant to be used for everyone irrespective of age, as the centuries wore on this extensive rite (which included catechumenal exorcisms and anointings and the three sacraments of initiation) was increasingly abbreviated, first in favor of infants and finally for everyone.

The upshot of all this was that by the time of the Second Vatican Council Catholic initiatory attitudes had come to focus on infants, and initiatory practice had been liturgically reduced to baptism and the ancillary rites immediately preceding and following it; catechumenal resonances had been shorn; confirmation and first communion were located elsewhere, the latter often preceding confirmation after Pope Saint Pius X in 1910 lowered the age for first communion to early childhood.[2] In the process several inadvertent reorientations occurred.

Reorientations of Initiatory Practice

First, catechesis was narrowed to programs of religious indoctrination by rote for children, represented by the *Baltimore Catechism* and other such products. The content was largely conceptual and invariably beyond a child's powers of real understanding; the recommended way of living a Christian life was predominantly focused on fulfilling requirements. Remembered answers to ill-understood questions and punctiliousness of observance thus became about all that most Catholics were given to live by. This did not produce a very evangelical or faith-mature community, but one strong on cohesion around approved practices, some of which were as fascinating as they were bizarre, devotional fads more or less sanctioned by authority. The ethos created was for the most part childish rather than childlike, apologetical rather than evangelical, both defensive and triumphalist, authoritarian rather than authoritative, and militant. It produced some splendid statistical results over a base that was in many ways brittle at its core.

Second, confirmation was cut loose from its frame of baptism and eucharist. Being restricted from its beginnings in the third century to the ministry of bishops (something insisted on by Pope Innocent I in 416), confirmation gradually separated from baptism as bishops became more unavailable in northern Europe during the Middle Ages. In many places local parishes were visited by their bishops only once or twice in a generation. This led to confirmation's falling into disuse in some areas, to its being only rarely administered in others, and then to children who were already approaching the age of canonical majority (the marriageable age of 16 for boys and 14 for girls). First communion was perforce delayed until such time. *All this meant in fact that active Christian life for many people did not begin until they were nominal adults.* Then they received confirmation, first communion, often marriage, sometimes religious vows and began going to confession. These sacraments and sacramentals, the first to be received since baptism in infancy, served not so much to initiate people into the church as into roles in a Christian society that included both church and state in an intimate symbiosis. Nominal adulthood was thus a time of high sacramental intensity: The Holy Spirit "revived" young people's baptism (an unremembered event in their lives) and communion regularized their lives as practicing Christians so that they could enter standard socioecclesiastical roles—the roles of the taxable, marriage and family, holy orders, religious vows. Confirmation "initiated" all this in the most solemn manner in the bishop's presence. Here is where the notion of confirmation as the sacrament of "maturity" began, and it rests on the abnormality of episcopal unavailability—abnormal because then the canonical age of confirmation was at baptism, and now at the age of reason.[3]

Third, the eucharist was reduced from its supreme position as the "seal of initiation" to the regularizing act by which the confirmed began to practice their faith on a *de jure* if not *de facto* adult level. Confirmation had come to overshadow both baptism and eucharist: Only a bishop could confirm, and this in what appeared to be extraordinary circumstances. An ordinary parish priest performed baptisms and presided at Mass all the time. Few people communicated much more often than once a year, when it was required during the Easter season. The sense of the eucharist as *communio* was thus not so strong as the sense of it as *sacrificium*—something people could see in the elevation of host and chalice, after the eleventh century, in a sort of "visual communion" as distinct from an actual sacramental communion, which was regarded as perhaps too awesome and perilous for one's soul to be undertaken often.

In very rough outline, what has been described is the disintegration of the components of Christian initiation, especially in catechesis and the sacraments of baptism, confirmation and eucharist. Baptism became the sacrament of Christian infancy, bringing with it basic salvation but no further active sacramental rights. Confirmation became the reactivator of baptism, the episcopally celebrated initiator of nominal Christian adulthood, supplier of Holy Spirit and the door into social and ecclesiastical observance. The eucharist became the symptom, anchor and touchstone of this practice on the adult level. Catechesis during childhood became the indoctrinational preparation for all this to begin.

These shifts are the ones that underlie much modern Catholic thought on confirmation and the initiation and catechesis of children. Part of our modern problems stem from not recognizing that the medieval shifts outlined previously were not about initiating *children* but about preparing and initiating nominal *adults* into punctilious observance of ritual and role obligations in a social and cultural complex that no longer exists. Ours is a new world in which Christian values are in decline and Christians are once again no longer a cognitive majority. The modern world, quite unlike the medieval, provides no clear and supportive roles to which many Christians feel obligated, and rituals of any but the secular sort are increasingly called into question, especially by the young. For such people the medieval paradigm of initiating nominal adults is precisely what is felt not to work. This is the main reason why confirmation programs unwittingly based on that paradigm often serve not to initiate the young more deeply into the church but to provide them with an exit from it. There are several reasons for this.

Confirmation as Exit from the Church

For one thing, modern young people, unlike their medieval counterparts, come to confirmation in late childhood or adolescence much more stimulated by secular media. The long period during which their baptism in infancy has lain dormant, except for a relatively brief period of indoctrination regarding practice preceding first communion in early childhood, has been filled with the patterns of behavior and the values of the modern post-Christian rather than of the medieval Christian world. Their personalities have already begun to set in these forms by the time they approach confirmation in adolescence. The appropriate catechesis would be to challenge and break down that personality-set; the appropriate sacramental seal to this would be solemn reconciliation to the church rather than confirmation. To think that a syllabus of studies followed by the sacrament of confirmation alone will accomplish this on a regular basis and for all is a serious underestimation of the power of the modern world. Exorcism is better here than education, and reconciliation tough and loving is better than confirmation into a socioecclesiastical world that no longer exists. Our era is more violent, bloody and oppressive than any in recorded history. Its power for ill on the developing personalities of children and their peer groups is appalling. A little education and oil on the forehead will not alleviate this power.

For another thing, there is no really evangelical dimension in either the medieval initiatory paradigm or in modern structures based on it. By "evangelical" one means proclaiming and manifesting the gospel of Jesus Christ to those *outside* the church. Those who, under grace, then come into the church by the conversion therapy of catechesis in the catechumenate and by sacramental initiation are the main agents of freshness in ecclesial perceptions. The church's converts help the church to avoid becoming stale and complacent; avoiding this state, the church is and can be seen to be *semper reformanda,* constantly reforming itself. This is the church's normal and healthy condition, a condition that the constant infusion of new blood from outside helps sustain.

Yet the church in this country baptizes 11 times more infants than it does adults, assuring that most of its catechetical programs are directed at already-baptized children and youth. In such a context, what evangelism there is tends toward the baptized faithful, completing an in-house circuit that risks staleness, complacency, a certain frustration and avoidance of the more daunting job of confronting the world with the gospel on the world's own grounds. In such a church, converts may sense less that they are welcomed and celebrated for the gifts they bring than that they are vaguely distrusted, not really part of the "group." Such a church may imperceptibly slide into solipsism: talking only to itself, committing the same mistakes, deepening the rut into which it continues to sink. Such a church prefers to evangelize itself rather than risk evangelizing the world. This is the most lethal risk of all.

One can see the continuing influence of the medieval paradigm in the fact that more than half the dioceses in this country confirm at ages 14 to 18, well after communion has begun to be received,[4] something even the medieval church did not do, and that is in fact discouraged if not entirely forbidden in the Council's initiatory reforms as well as in the 1983 Code of Canon Law.[5] Such confirmation practice takes the sacrament out of its initiatory context, making it a renewal of baptismal vows and a rite of passage into cultural adulthood. If this is still "initiatory," then confirmation, not eucharist, becomes the "seal of initiation" about which the tradition, the conciliar reforms and the 1983 Code speak. What one is seeing here is a shift of an initiatory sacrament into youth therapy that then becomes *de facto* the "seal of initiation," displacing the eucharist.[6]

It is no wonder that such a convolution confuses sacramental intelligibility and produces a catechesis in disarray as well as a possibly warped sense of Christian identity. All this is intensified as this usage and catechesis of confirmation is found in practice to serve as an opportunity for youth to *leave* the church more often than to enter it more deeply, as many hope. It cannot be ruled out that young people are more acute in getting the point than their catechists and pastors.

Restore the Order

This contradiction is what arises when the evangelical dynamic of Christian initiation turns inward on itself and sacramental syntax is ignored. The 1972 Rite of Christian Initiation of Adults (RCIA) attempts to set the syntax straight once again by insisting that Christian initiation is about bringing the God-given grace of conversion to ecclesial term by evangelization, catechesis (as conversion therapy) and the sacraments of initiation—baptism, confirmation and eucharist *in that order.* All other forms of initiation, such as reception of persons from other churches and the delayed completion of initiation for those previously baptized, are to take the adult sequence as the norm and inspiration for all the adaptations in other cases as may be required, including children.

This means that all who come to full initiation in the Catholic church must have their faith in the gospel assured at some point by evangelical scrutiny to the fullest extent possible. That faith must then be brought to ecclesial term by tough and loving catechesis that focuses on the church's sacraments of initiation in the right order, always consummated in the eucharist, the seal of initiation. This is the modest and normal structure that is meant to be filled out with care, love and wisdom as circumstances allow by courageous evangelists, discerning catechesis and good pastors and parents. The structure provides perspective and coherence to the entire endeavor, which is at the very heart of the church's existence and mission in the world and from which issues a Christian identity that is firm and clear. The structure is not an idol but a coherent standard, supple and adaptable, for how the company of believers goes about its fundamental business of bringing all people to stand in Christ before his Father by the Holy Spirit.

The initiatory norm applies to children no less than to adults. It means that they must be evangelized as they become capable, catechized so as to bring their nascent faith by appropriate stages to ecclesial term and (for those already baptized in infancy) initiated fully by confirmation and first holy communion in that order. One of the main principles in the RCIA is that one cannot proceed *a priori* in matters of catechesis: The endeavor must go according to the abilities of the catechumen. For some children it may go more slowly or rapidly than for others, and it should not be governed by peer group pressure, education grade level, age categories or ecclesiastical administrators who want to keep everything tidy. Symmetry and conformity are not nearly so important as nurturing the seeds of grace, a ministry that cannot be rushed or over-ridden. This is a common mistake that betrays a lack of discernment among catechists and risks turning out nominal Christians more fixed on conforming to others' expectations than on faith owned and viable. Graduating from some grade in school says no more about the quality of a child's faith and Christian identity than changing jobs says about the same factors for an adult. It is of the essence that catechists, parents and pastors not forget this. Programmatic, ideological or educational regimentation cannot obtain or direct the curious ways in which grace often works. It is to grace in the initiate that the church in its catechesis and sacraments must be appropriately obedient and faithful at whatever age.

Parenting, Pastoring, Preaching

Nor does the history of initiating children allow one to forget how indispensable parents are in the catechetical endeavor. Monica's example, prayer and immense patience, including no doubt a good bit of hectoring, eventually brought her son Augustine to sacramental initiation when he was an adult in his 30s. For worse or better, parents are inevitably their children's first catechists in faith. This counsels that catechists and pastors would do well to expend as much effort in supporting parents of children in their catechetical efforts as they expend on the children themselves. Institutional catechesis often can be rendered ineffective if children have been previously left uncatechized or miscatechized by parents who are themselves consumed by an unchristian culture and virtually without Christian values in their homes. One meets such children and such parents, alas, all the time.

This is one area in which the parish Sunday liturgy superbly done can be of great help. However else one might describe such a liturgy, it simply must have a greater psychic impact and a more powerful cultural attraction on both children and their parents than a visit to the local shopping mall or discount store. Even the best catechists and pastors cannot serve their people if the people are not motivated to desire those services and to make themselves available for them. They will surely not be very motivated if the standard fare they find in their parish is a less powerful factor in their lives than what this world that passes offers them. They will seek power where they find it. Poor liturgy and poor preaching of the gospel render both the catechetical and pastoral tasks all but impossible. And when these tasks fail, the great evangelical mission of the church in the modern world lapses. The church itself becomes little more than a refuge for idealists who produce nothing, like a small nation with high morals but no production to enable it to pay its bills.

Christian initiation is about bringing converts to God in Christ by the Spirit under grace, no matter where those converts come from or what age they may be. Courageous evangelism, discerning catechesis, gospel preaching and splendid public worship are symptoms as well as causes of a firm Christian identity and self-confidence that stem only from a faith well owned for the life of the world. Such a faith is never childish, but it is childlike, for as it is written, "a little child shall lead them." But what a Child this One has turned out to be.

NOTES

1. See my *The Shape of Baptism: The Rites of Christian Initiation* (New York: Pueblo Publishing Company, 1978), 54–67.

2. Ibid., 69–70.

3. See my *Confirmation: Origins and Reform* (New York: Pueblo Publishing Company, 1988), 81–118.

4. See Paul Turner, *The Meaning and Practice of Confirmation* (New York: Peter Lang, Inc., 1987), 317–18.

5. Michael J. Balhoff, "Age for Confirmation: Canonical Evidence," *The Jurist,* 45:2 (1985): 549–87.

6. In 1986 the diocese of Columbus, Ohio, polled 149 clergy, parents, DREs, teachers and others on initiatory questions. On the statement, "The sacrament that completes Christian initiation is the eucharist," 71 agreed while 68

disagreed. On the statement, "First eucharist before confirmation is to be the preferred sequence," 92 agreed while only 34 disagreed. See Rita Fisher, "Columbus Confirmation Survey," *Liturgical Apostolate: Newsletter of the Office of Liturgy, Diocese of Columbus* 23:2 (1988): 1–2. For the entirely novel notion of confirmation as a "remembering [sic] of eucharist," see Arthur J. Kubick, "Confirmation at St. Elizabeth Parish: A Reflection," *Catechumenate* 10 (November 1988): 36–43.

CHAPTER
4

"*It is the community that makes God's love real and concrete to the child and provides the sense of belonging that is basic to baptism. The child learns to pray, forgive, celebrate and serve in the midst of a people who pray, forgive, celebrate and serve.***"**

Baptismal Catechesis for Children of Catechetical Age

CATHERINE DOOLEY

Patty is 9 years old and attends the public school in her area where many of her school friends are Catholics. Patty asked her mother to take her to the church that her friends attend. Patty's mother is a divorced, single parent who was baptized in a Roman Catholic church but has not been active for many years. Surviving a divorce and providing for her child have taken up much of her time and energy in the past years. She did take Patty to the parish church and was surprised by the warm welcome she received from the parents of Patty's friends, from the associate pastor and from the religious education staff. Within a few months, she asked that Patty be prepared for the sacraments of initiation.

A Chinese couple enrolled their child in a Catholic school. They had no objection to the child's participating in the religion classes but made it clear that they did not intend to accept Christianity. The child is now in seventh grade, and his sister is in the first grade. The mother recently asked for baptism for herself and for her children. The fact that the oldest child wanted to be baptized was one factor in the mother's decision, but another was the mother's experience of a sense of belonging and acceptance within the school community.

These are two examples of the growing number of unbaptized children of catechetical age who ask for initiation. In the past, unbaptized children often were looked on as somewhat of a problem because they needed special instruction in order to join the catechetical classes appropriate to their age level. The concern was the doctrinal "catch-up" required so that they would "fit" into their peer group. Generally, it was an awkward situation for everyone involved—child, parent and catechist. The sacramental initiation, held as unobtrusively as possible in order to avoid embarrassment for the children or their families, often communicated a certain second-class status. In other words, pastoral practice countered the theology of initiation.

In contrast, the Rite of Christian Initiation of Adults (RCIA), accommodated to children, affirms the role of the community in the formation of children. In mandating the implementation of the RCIA in every parish in the United States, the National Conference of Catholic Bishops recommends that the formation of unbaptized children of catechetical age "should follow the general pattern of the ordinary catechumenate as far as possible, with the appropriate adaptation permitted by the ritual."[1] The introduction to the children's order notes that the children's growth in faith depends on the help and example of their companions and on the influence of their parents (RCIA, 254). Children within the same situation should be grouped together for the celebrations of the rites in order that they may help one another to grow in faith. Representatives of the Christian community, both adults and the children's peer group, should actively participate in these celebrations so that the children can experience the meaning of belonging to a Christian community.

The introduction indicates that the unbaptized children should be assimilated into their peer group as much as possible but offers several reservations or cautions. First, conversion cannot be programmed.

> Christian initiation of children requires both a conversion that is personal and somewhat developed, in proportion to their age and the assistance of the education they need. The process of initiation thus must be adapted both to their spiritual progress, that

is, to the children's growth in faith and to the catechetical instruction they receive. (RCIA, 253)

Secondly, while some aspects of the catechetical instruction of the children's peer group may be appropriately shared with catechumens of catechetical age before their reception of the sacraments of confirmation and eucharist, nevertheless "their condition and status as catechumens should not be compromised or confused, nor should they receive the sacraments of initiation in any sequence other than that determined in the ritual of Christian initiation" (National Statutes, 19), that is, confirmation follows baptism and precedes eucharist.

This chapter focuses on catechesis for children of catechetical age. Because the catechumenate is the pattern for formation,[2] the *first* part of the chapter will outline the principles of catechesis found in the introduction to the RCIA. The *second* part will focus on the element of catechetical instruction by taking a brief look at the approaches of the great catechists of Christian antiquity as a possible source of direction for contemporary baptismal catechesis.

Principles of Catechesis

Gradual Process. The introduction to the RCIA, 75, provides basic principles of catechesis for initiation into the church. The emphasis in the RCIA is on a gradual formation, a spiritual journey, that is adapted to the needs, age, culture and capability of those being initiated. The gradual growth in faith is recognized and nurtured within the structure of the catechumenate itself. Initiation includes several steps marked by liturgical rites. Periods of formation lead up to and follow the steps of their initiation (253). The duration of the catechumenate is not determined beforehand but depends on children's growth in faith as well as personal and family circumstances. The initiation may extend over several years, but a yearlong catechumenate may be sufficient for the children who have the opportunity to join the parish or school catechetical programs for an extended mystagogy.

Paschal Character. The whole initiation is to bear a markedly paschal character, for the initiation of Christians is the first sacramental sharing in Christ's dying and rising. In addition, the period of purification and enlightenment ordinarily coincides with Lent; the celebration of the sacraments is at the Easter Vigil;[3] and the period of postbaptismal catechesis (mystagogy) coincides with the Easter season.

Conversion is the aim of this process of formation. Conversion is "the profound change of the whole person by which one *begins* to consider, judge and arrange one's life according to the holiness and love of God" made manifest in Jesus and given to one in abundance (Rite of Penance, 6a). Conversion means that the death and resurrection of Jesus are the paradigm of the Christian's life, and the Christian commits herself or himself to the daily struggle of moving from death to life, from selfishness to love and from sin to grace.

For children of catechetical age, the awareness of God in their lives will be gradual and will be consonant with their level of development. Obviously, it will be different for the eight-year-old child and the 15-year-old adolescent. The awakening to faith will correspond to the individual's growing ability to recognize that God's love is the source of life, and the purpose of life is found in God's call.

Community. The initiation of children into the Christian community and life is primarily the responsibility of parents and of the community as community. Both examples given at the beginning of this chapter indicate the importance of welcoming communities.

In the case of unbaptized children of catechetical age, the parents, often for a variety of reasons, are able only minimally to support their children in the journey of faith. The peer group will be an important element in the children's progress in faith, as well as the adult members of the community who act as sponsors, godparents and catechists. The whole community must be aware of its importance in the children's formation because children learn more from what adults do than from what they say. The children's sacramental initiation depends on ordinary experiences within the community. It is the community that makes God's love real and concrete to the children and provides the sense of belonging that is basic to baptism. The children learn to pray, forgive, celebrate and serve in the midst of a people who pray, forgive, celebrate and serve.

Mission. The process of formation brings with it a progressive change of outlook and conduct that should become manifest by means of its social consequences (RCIA, 75.2), that is, the catechumen should learn to work actively with others in the coming of God's reign through service to others. Baptism, confirmation and eucharist are directed to mission. Young children at their level of development are only beginning to go beyond themselves in care and concern for others. A variety of realistic and appropriate ways of service must be opened up to them. Primarily, the children need to share in the concrete actions of concern for the hungry, for the environment or for peace that are the concerns of the family or the adult sponsors. The actions and attitudes of the adults will speak most clearly to the children about care for the elderly and for the homeless or the need to conserve the world's resources.

Liturgical Formation. The primary formative experience for the catechumens is the liturgy, particularly the liturgical rites of the RCIA. The church gathered in worship shapes the identity and the faith of the catechumens and the baptized in the very act of celebration. Worship expresses and creates the church, and the church at worship manifests and constitutes the church. In sacred liturgy, the individual and the community worship God as an assembly called by God, and the words and gestures deepen the awareness of who they are and what they are to become.

In a coherent way, the liturgical celebrations of the RCIA develop the basic ritual signs that are part of all Christian celebrations: gathering of the assembly; signing with the cross; proclaiming the word; laying on of hands; anointing; illuminating; being immersed into water and sharing the eucharistic bread and wine. The rites build on the human experiences of children—"activity of the community, exchange of greetings, capacity to listen and to seek and grant pardon, expression of gratitude, experience of symbolic actions, a meal of friendship and festive celebration"[4]—and do not need to be explained. Children intuit the association even though their ability to articulate the meaning may be limited. The task of catechesis is to explore these signs, to look at their origins in the story of salvation for insight into their meaning in celebration and Christian life. These ritual signs are primary forms of catechesis in which the whole community takes part. They speak to the memory and to the imagination and give the children, as it were, a "vocabulary," a language of faith, that opens up and unfolds into a way of life. The ritual signs are a powerful, nonverbal form of catechesis that are experienced rather than explained. The rite states that the catechesis of the catechumens should be adapted to the liturgical cycle of the church year and should be enriched by celebrations of the word. All catechetical instruction should take place in the context of prayer (84).

Catechetical Instruction. In light of these principles, the catechumenate is not a "mere exposition of dogmatic truths and norms of morality but a period of formation in the whole Christian life."[5] The focus is on conversion, so the instruction during the catechumenate is not an end in itself but is directed to worship and to mission. Within this context of prayer and celebrations of the word, the message is communicated through scripture, liturgy and faith actively expressed and lived in the church. At first glance it may seem that this catechumenal approach, with its emphasis on experience of Christian living, is incompatible with the call for a "systematic" catechesis, dealing with essentials, sufficiently complete and open to all other factors of the Christian life.[6] Still, the structure of the catechumenate may provide the best means of achieving these goals, because it does not compartmentalize one element of the total catechesis from another.

On a practical level, however, many catechists find themselves sounding like the deacon, Deogratias, who wrote to St.

Augustine asking for concrete suggestions about a catechesis for the inquirers. In this search for a way to develop baptismal catechesis, I would like to underline Agnes Cunningham's assertion that "on the question of baptismal catechesis, the early church fathers are preeminent guides and mentors"[7] and suggest that the great catechists of the early catechumenate offer an approach that would be well worth examining for contemporary practice.

Catechesis in the Tradition

Inquirers. St. Augustine's approach to catechesis was through the *enarratio* or exposition of sacred history.[8] He instructed the catechist to present to the inquirer the whole account of God's intervention in human history that later would be unfolded for the candidates in liturgical worship for the rest of their lives. In commenting on Augustine's "First Catechetical Instruction," Gerard Sloyan notes that the plan was effective because there was a full-scale exposition of the sacred books. Otherwise the candidate gets bits and pieces of the scripture but has no overall context in which to place the specific teaching.[9] Augustine's catechesis always began with some experience of daily life, some longing of the human heart or some fear that bound the individual. For Augustine, the proclamation of God's mighty deeds had only one purpose: that the inquirers might know how much they are loved by God and from the knowledge of this truth "might begin to glow with the love of God by which one is loved and therefore might love one's neighbor in the example of Christ who made himself our neighbor by loving us." Augustine says that there is nothing that invites love more than to be loved. Even those who are the most unwilling to give love, would be willing to return love. Augustine's admonition to catechists is that God's love for us is to be the reference point for everything that they might say so that those "to whom you speak by hearing may believe, and by believing may hope and by hoping may love."[10]

After the instruction, the candidates were asked if they believed what they had heard. If they freely assented, they were received into the catechumenate by what Augustine called the *sacramenta:* "The signing with the cross was a shadow of baptism, the laying on of hands a shadow of confirmation, while the handing over of bread and salt was a shadow of the eucharist that was to come."[11]

These signs were the language of faith by which one entered into the mysteries of Christ. The catechumen and the neophyte were formed in the gospel not only by instruction but by liturgical rites and apostolic endeavors.

Catechumens. In fourth-century Jerusalem, the catechumens each day during Lent were first exorcised and then given three hours of instruction on the scriptures, the resurrection and faith. During the last two weeks of Lent, the bishop explained the creed, article by article in the same way in which he had presented the scriptures.[12] The catechumens, in turn, were expected to learn the creed by heart to be able to "give it back," that is, to recite it publicly as a profession of faith and a chant of praise for all that God has done. The creed put in summary form the story of salvation that had been the content of the catechumens' instruction for several preceding years.

Thirteen of the 18 catechetical homilies of Cyril of Jerusalem focus on the creed of Jerusalem.[13] All of the instructions contain solid doctrine, but Christian doctrine was never an end in itself. It was always directed to the deepening of the covenant relationship with God. Its source was scripture and its expression was worship.

Mystagogy. The mystagogical catechesis took place after the sacraments had been experienced.[14] The experience of the liturgy was the source of the postbaptismal catechesis, and the fathers of the church believed that the rite itself brings insight. In the experience of initiation, the neophytes have been enlightened and brought to a new vision of the Christian mysteries. The great mystagogues described this sacramental experience almost exclusively in scriptural images. The bread of the eucharist was compared with the manna in the desert; baptism is prefigured in the crossing of the Reed Sea, in the flood, in the healing of the paralytic in the pool of Bethsaida, so that the neophytes might recognize the unity of God's word and work.[15] For the mystagogues, the events in the story of salvation were not only manifestations of God's presence in the past but the actions of God now in the sacramental life of the church. The word proclaims and effects salvation; the sacraments express and effect salvation.

The readings, the catechetical instructions and the homilies of the early church provided the catechumens and all the faithful with an extensive knowledge of the scripture. The use of biblical images to probe the sacramental experience was a powerful way of communicating meaning. The scriptures gave the people the key to understanding liturgical language and to participating in the sacred mysteries. The formative influence of the liturgy brought about the transformation of the Christians and of their society.

These few examples from the patristic writings offer a vision of Christian catechesis that shows the integral relationship of all of its sources: scripture, liturgy, doctrine and life.[17] The catechesis had only one aim: that the catechumens might come to love God in Christ and to live this love in service to others.

Direction for Contemporary Catechesis?

In light of the patristic approach and the principles of the introduction to the RCIA, what are the elements to be included in the catechetical instruction for each of the periods of the catechumenal process?

The Precatechumenate. The task of the community in the period of the precatechumenate is evangelization: to proclaim faithfully and constantly the living God and Jesus Christ who has been sent for the salvation of all (RCIA, 36). The aim is to awaken faith in and to foster a relationship with the living God present and active within this community of believers. Beginning with a theology of the word and a brief introduction to how the scriptures are formed (appropriate to the child's age level), the *enarratio* (exposition of the story of salvation) of the period of evangelization or precatechumenate could explore the mystery of God's love as it is manifested in creation, revealed in the events of Israel and expressed most fully in the death and resurrection of Jesus Christ. Jesus continues to be present in the church through the working of the Holy Spirit, calling the community of believers to holiness and faithfulness.

For us, as for Augustine, the *enarratio* is not history but God's self-revelation to humankind. Augustine saw the sacraments as one more aspect of the plan of salvation. Just as the creation and the events of the Exodus and Sinai are manifestations of God's presence, so, too, are the sacraments. This revelation calls for a free response of faith that is expressed in words and deeds. Each of these stories of salvation is like a piece of a mosaic that when assembled vividly portrays the images— God's call, the human response in love, belonging to the community of believers, identification by name, the journey of faith, marking with the cross, and the power of the word—that are the dominant themes and gestures in the Rite of Acceptance into the Order of Catechumens. If these stories and images have been celebrated in prayer and in ritual gesture week by week, the children will truly know what it means to "come into the land I will show you" and to proclaim "this is the lamb of God. We have found the Messiah."

The Catechumenate. The introduction to the RCIA directs that the instruction that the catechumens receive during this period presents Catholic teaching in its entirety, enlightens faith, directs the heart toward God, fosters participation in the liturgy, inspires apostolic activity and nurtures a life completely in accord with the spirit of Christ (RCIA, 78). Catechetical instruction should take into account the liturgical seasons and should be supported by celebrations of the word so that the instruction is always held within the context of prayer (84).

The *praenotanda,* rites, prayers and lectionary are again the sources of catechesis. The catechist looks to the celebration of the word of God, the minor exorcisms, blessings, anointings and the presentations of the creed and the Lord's Prayer for a rich catechesis of word and sign. The meetings of the catechumens after the Sunday liturgy of the word focus on the passages of the lectionary and may also include an exorcism or a blessing. Because, for pastoral reasons, the RCIA allows the presentation of the creed and the Lord's Prayer to take place during the period of the catechumenate, the creed and the Lord's Prayer form the major part of the catechesis. The creed is presented in its trinitarian structure in the broader context of creation, redemption and sanctification. As Berard Marthaler notes, the baptismal creeds were originally a narrative. They told the story of the saving events that are the basis for the faith of the Christian community.

> The three parts of the story tell of God's action in creation, in Jesus of Nazareth and in the Spirit who continues to work in the life and history of church. The narrative function of the creed is most evident in the second part, which tells of Jesus' heavenly origins, his birth, life, death and resurrection.[18]

The creed summarizes the main points of the kerygma and recounts the saving events that are the foundation of the faith of the Christian community.

Purification and Enlightenment. The catechesis during this more intense period of preparation, coinciding with Lent, is taken preferably from the lectionary readings of Cycle A. These Sunday readings speak of conversion and renewal. The first Sundays of Lent remind the catechumens of the meaning of this period of their formation. The readings focus on the temptations of Jesus (purification) and his transfiguration (enlightenment). The readings of the third, fourth and fifth Sundays from the Gospel of John unfold the baptismal symbols of water, light and life. In addition to the celebration of the liturgy of the word, the penitential rites (evangelical scrutinies) are occasions of major catechesis in which the whole community takes part. The children's order notes that the penitential rites have a similar purpose to the evangelical scrutinies in the adult rite (RCIA, 291) and the guidelines for the scrutinies may be followed and adapted. This norm should be kept in mind, because the penitential rite for children seems to be as concerned with baptized children who may be receiving the sacrament of penance for the first time (RCIA, 293, 295, 298, 299, 303) as with catechumens who are entering more deeply and fully into the process of Christian conversion.

Mystagogy. The lectionary readings of the Easter season, especially Cycle A, are the source of catechesis. A central image from each of the Sunday readings[19] can deepen the meaning of what already has been experienced in ritual and prayer. The images of the light, the breaking of the bread and the shepherd put the baptismal covenant relationship in clearer focus. The approach of the fathers of the church—developing the memory and the imagination of the neophytes—opens the way to deeper insight into the mystery of God's faithful and gracious love present in their lives.

Conclusion

This chapter has attempted to lay out the principles that underlie the formation of children through the catechumenate. Catechumenal catechesis is a process of integrating scripture, liturgy and doctrine that takes place within the community of faith and opens that community to the coming reign of God. Catechetical instruction is but one aspect of this process. Catechesis involves not only cognitive thought, content and memory but also imagination, action and transformation. Catechesis, in the context of the celebrations of the word of God (RCIA, 82), has the purpose of implanting in the hearts of children the teachings they receive; helping them experience different aspects of prayer; enabling them to enter into the signs, celebrations and seasons of the liturgy; preparing them to participate fully in the worship assembly of the larger community and calling that entire assembly to new life.

The development of a children's catechumenate is only in an incipient stage. Pastors and catechists are looking for models of implementation. One of the most valuable sources of insight and inspiration is to be found in the catechetical tradition of Augustine, Ambrose and Cyril of Jerusalem.

NOTES

1. National Statutes for the Catechumenate, 17. *Documentation for General Meeting,* National Conference of Catholic Bishops (Washington, D.C.: United States Catholic Conference, 1986).

2. The "Message to the People of God" of the 1977 Synod of Bishops on *Catechesis in Our Times* calls the catechumenate "the model" for all catechesis (*Living Light* 15 [Spring 1978]: 91); also, *Sharing the Light of Faith,* 115 (Washington, D.C.: United States Catholic Conference, 1979), 67, states that the catechumenate provides the norm for all catechetical as well as liturgical practice with regard to initiation.

3. The text of RCIA, 304 states: "preferably at the Easter Vigil or on a Sunday." For pastoral reasons, some presiders prefer not to baptize children at the Easter Vigil and provision is made for this in RCIA, 306. In the early church, the vigil of Pentecost was a second occasion for initiation. See J. D. C. Fisher, *Christian Initiation: Baptism in the Medieval West* (London: SPCK, 1965), 3.

4. *Directory for Masses with Children,* 9 (Washington, D.C.: United States Catholic Conference, 1974).

5. *Decree on the Church's Missionary Activity,* 14 (Washington, D.C.: United States Catholic Conference, 1965).

6. Pope John Paul II, "*Catechesi Tradendae:* Apostolic Exhortation on Catechesis," 21 (Washington, D.C.: United States Catholic Conference, 1979). See also Mary A. Fitzsimmons, "Systematic Catechesis in the RCIA," *Living Light* 17 (Winter 1980): 321–26.

7. Agnes Cunningham, "Patristic Catechesis for Baptism: A Pedagogy for Christian Living" in *Before and After Baptism,* ed. James A. Wilde (Chicago: Liturgy Training Publications, 1988), 15–25.

8. Augustine of Hippo, "The First Catechetical Instruction," *Ancient Christian Writers* 2, trans. Joseph P. Christopher (New York: Newman Press, 1946).

9. Gerard Sloyan makes the comment that Augustine's plan is effective only because there is a full-scale exposition of the sacred books. "Otherwise the Bible becomes a tantalizing conundrum without historical context or literal sense of its own. He uses the scripture narratives in his initial instruction to whet spiritual appetites, but the technique is valid only so long as the appetite has a chance of being later satisfied. Otherwise the candidate will receive nothing but an incomplete and garbled ladling out of biblical information." In "Religious Education: From Early Christianity to Medieval Times," in *Shaping the Christian Message,* ed. Gerard Sloyan (New York: The MacMillan Company, 1958), 20.

10. "The First Catechetical Instruction," 23–24.

11. F. Van Der Meer, *Augustine the Bishop,* trans. B. Battershaw and G. R. Lamb (New York: Sheed and Ward, 1961), 354.

12. John Wilkinson, ed. *Egeria's Travels to the Holy Land* (Jerusalem: Ariel Publishing House, 1981), 126.

13. Cyril of Jerusalem, "Catechetical Lectures," in *A Select Library of Nicene and Post-Nicene Fathers of the Christian Church* 7, second series, trans. Philip Schaff and Henry Wace (Grand Rapids: William B. Eerdmans, 1983).

14. See Mary Pierre Ellebracht, "Today This Word Has Been Fulfilled in Your Midst," *Worship* 60 (July 1986): 347–61, for an enlightening discussion of St. Ambrose's *De Mysteriis* on this point.

15. For a new look at typology, see Gail Ramshaw, "Stories to Image God" in *Liturgy* 7/1 (1987): 75–79.

16. Josef Jungmann, "The Role of the Liturgy in the Transformation of Pagan Society," *The Early Liturgy* (Notre Dame: Notre Dame University Press, 1959), 164–74.

17. For an excellent discussion of patristic catechesis, see Walter Burghardt, "Catechetics in the Early Church: Program and Psychology" in *Living Light* 1 (Autumn 1964): 100–18.

18. Berard Marthaler, *The Creed* (Mystic: Twenty-Third Publications, 1987), 9–11.

19. A valuable source for this catechesis is *An Easter Sourcebook: The Fifty Days,* ed. Gabe Huck, Gail Ramshaw and Gordon Lathrop (Chicago: Liturgy Training Publications, 1988); another rich mystagogical resource developing the images and themes of Eastertime and other parts of the church calendar is *At That Time: Cycles and Seasons in the Life of a Christian,* ed. James A. Wilde (Chicago: Liturgy Training Publications, 1989).

CHAPTER

5

"How much does a child or adult need to 'know' in order to be accepted into the Christian community? How do we teach 'doctrine' to children—or to anyone?"

The Creed and Doctrine in Catechesis for Children

BERARD L. MARTHALER

How much does a child or adult need to "know" in order to be accepted into the Christian community? How do we teach "doctrines" to children — or to anyone? These issues are not new to catechists; they can be resolved by reference to precedents that go back to the earliest days of the church. Let us begin with the second question because the answer to the first depends on our understanding of doctrine.

Sometime around the year 420 an unknown inquirer, Laurentius by name, wrote to the renowned bishop of Hippo, requesting that he furnish him with a handbook of Christian doctrine. Augustine wondered about the usefulness of the exercise. "You have," he wrote, "the creed and the Lord's Prayer. What can be briefer to hear or to read? What is easier to commit to memory?"

Despite his misgivings, the great doctor composed a handbook *(enchiridion),* a treatise on faith, hope and charity. It was nothing else than an explanation of the creed, the Lord's Prayer and the twofold commandment, love of God and love of neighbor. "What we are to believe, what we are to hope for, and what we are to love," according to Augustine, is the sum total of Christian doctrine.[1] Like other medieval figures before and after him,

Thomas Aquinas adopted the Augustinian outline for the catechetical instructions that he gave in the last year of his life. It formed the basic structure of catechesis into modern times.

The Creed

The heart of catechesis for Augustine was the baptismal creed. (The wording of the creed used in North Africa was substantially the same as the later version that we have come to know as the Apostles' Creed.) It was the topic of sermons that he delivered to catechumens. It was the basis of a discourse he delivered to his fellow bishops in which he said,

> We have . . . the catholic faith in the creed, known to the faithful and committed to memory in a form of expression as concise as has been rendered admissible by the circumstances of the case; the purpose of which [compilation] was, that individuals who are but beginners and sucklings among those who have been born again in Christ, and who have not yet been strengthened by most diligent and spiritual handling and understanding of the divine scriptures, should be furnished with a summary, expressed in a few words, of those matters of necessary belief that were subsequently to be explained to them in many words, as they made progress.[2]

The sure and proper foundation of faith is Christ. For Augustine the trinitarian structure of the creed is the key, the basis for any summary of doctrine. He identified "those matters of necessary belief" with the history of salvation. The work of the Triune God in the world—creation, redemption and sanctification—is the essence of the story, everything else is simply detail.

For Augustine baptism was not a question of knowledge, but of faith and commitment. When catechumens accepted the story as *true* and were willing to bring their lives into conformity to the example of Christ and the norms of the church, they were initiated into the community. Living out that faith and baptismal commitment became the task of a lifetime.

Apostolic preaching—the kerygma—was even more succinct. The initial call to faith proclaimed: "Christ died for our sins in accordance with the scriptures"; "he was buried"; "he was raised to life on the third day in accordance with the scriptures" (1 Corinthians 15:3–4); and "God has made him both Lord and Christ, this Jesus whom you crucified" (Acts 2:36). Implicit in this initial proclamation was an affirmation of the divine mission of Jesus and a call to live the Christian life. Those who accepted the message were baptized.

It is faith in the person and work of Jesus that saves. St. Paul gives his own brief summary of salvation history in Romans 5:15, 18–19:

> Though it was through one person that sin and death entered the world, how much more did the grace of God and the gracious gift of one person, Jesus Christ, abound for all. . . . To sum up: Just as a single offense brought condemnation to all, a single right-eous act brought acquittal and life to all. Just as through one person's disobedience all became sinners, so through one person's obedience all shall become just.

There is probably no more concise statement of Christian doctrine than the above. The mystery of evil and the promise of justification, the theology of sin and salvation, are packed into a few short phrases. Tomes have been written to explain them, but Christian theology is, at root, nothing more than an elab-oration of the stories that have traditionally been told about Adam and Eve, and the passion, death and resurrection of Jesus Christ. They are stories that children and illiterate adults can appreciate, can believe, even when they do not grasp the underlying philosophical and theological issues.

Catechists initiate individuals—children and adults—into the church by telling the story in word and sacrament and by helping them, in whatever way humans can, to respond to the workings of the Holy Spirit in their lives. The story is told and retold, sometimes briefly, sometimes at length, but it is always the same. This is the belief of the Christian community, the doctrine of the church. There is no other. At the point that a catechumen affirms the creedal articles of creation, redemp-tion and sanctification, he or she is ready to identify with the church. Someone may become more knowledgeable about the Bible, gain a better grasp of ritual, be able to outline church history and explain canon law, but that individual will never be more justified than when he or she for the first time confesses that Jesus Christ is Lord and believes in the heart that God raised him or her from the dead. "Faith in the heart leads to justification," wrote Paul. "Confession on the lips, to salvation" (Romans 10:9–10).

Doctrine and Lists of Doctrines

Just as horticulturists can number and catalog trees without attending to whether they are observing the trees in a nursery or a forest, it is possible to list doctrines without ever coming to grips with the foundation of Christian doctrine, the kerygma.

When theology is divorced from the kerygma, when teaching and learning doctrine becomes an end in itself, the catechetical task is perverted and the very mission of the church threatened. In the second century, gnostic sects claimed secret knowledge, inside information that came by special revelation known only to the initiated. They presented this knowledge *(gnosis)* as the source and means of salvation. The deeper one was immersed into the arcane mysteries, the closer one came to union with the divine. The gnostics established an elite, a hierarchy of believers based on knowledge. The church in the person of Saint Irenaeus of Lyons and others reacted strongly. They denounced the position that salvation is based on knowledge or that there is a freestanding body of doctrine, a corpus of teachings that have a life of their own apart from the faith of the Christian community. (It always has been assumed that someone poorly informed may nonetheless be strong in faith.)

The gnostic tendency, deeply rooted in the human psyche, continues to tempt the modern church. Lists of doctrines, basic teachings, outstanding elements of the Christian message and guidelines for doctrinal soundness may serve a purpose, but it is important to understand what that purpose is. In the twelfth century Hugh of Saint Victor compiled lists of seven: seven deadly sins, seven petitions of the Lord's Prayer, seven gifts of the Holy Spirit, seven principal virtues and seven beatitudes— to aid the memory.[3] In the fifteenth century Jean Gerson wrote

"ABCs for Simple Folk." It incorporated Hugh of St. Victor's lists of seven, the Ten Commandments, the works of mercy and other items a Christian should know, but it too was intended as mnemonic device. It was a means, not an end in itself. Modern lists, however, sometimes take on a life of their own. They are used as checklists for completeness (a practical purpose), as tests for orthodoxy (an impractical purpose) and as ways of measuring the success (or, more often, of demonstrating the failure) of catechetical programs. Inventories of religious education outcomes based on these lists measure knowledge, not piety nor reverence, not religious practice nor commitment.

It is unrealistic to deny the fascination that lists provide. They are useful insofar as they help organize data and systematize information, but they are dysfunctional when people are more intent on memorizing the lists than trying to understand and interpret the data. Wisdom is more than information retrieval and mastery of facts. The purpose of catechesis is not to prepare children to play Trivial Pursuit when they grow older but to nurture their faith so that it "becomes living, explicit and productive through formation in doctrine and the experience of Christian living" *(Code of Canon Law, 773).*

To illustrate what we mean by doctrine, Gerald O'Collins of Gregorian University draws three concentric circles. He marks the largest circle on the outer rim, "church life," and the inmost circle, the smallest, "dogmas." The middle circle represents church doctrine. "Everything that Christians believe, confess and teach," he says, "can be labeled doctrine."[4] The outer circle is intended to illustrate that the full range of Christian life and activity is greater than church doctrine.

If one were to master a comprehensive list of Catholic teachings without being active in a church community, one would miss a good deal that is essential to the spirit and forms of Catholicism. Recently E. D. Hirsch, Jr., popularized a list of patriotic lore, historical events, famous people and geographical names that literate Americans should know. It is a catalog of terms that appear in newspapers, magazines and books without explanation. The list covers a range from sports to theater, from current events to biblical allusions; it includes words and phrases that one hears on the radio and uses in conversation and everyday discourse (and which one needs to have in mind when working crossword puzzles). The terms, however, have little value in themselves, apart from the fabric of American culture. They are like so many threads that need to be woven into cloth for them to take on any significance that transcends the raw material of which they are made. "To understand what somebody is saying," writes Hirsch, "we must understand more than the surface meaning of words; we have to understand the context as well."[5]

The Communal Context of Faith

The context for religious literacy is the Christian community. There is the liturgy that brings people together to hear the word and break bread. Icons and music give expression to shared beliefs. Values are held in common. Service of various kinds is regarded as a duty and hallmark of the group as well as of individual members. The tradition has shaped ethnic and family practices that are handed from generation to generation. Theology, canon law, papal teachings, devotions, religious education programs, the parochial school and every aspect of parish life provide the context for Catholic culture. When divorced from the life of the community, doctrine is like a tapestry hanging in a museum rather than a fabric to be worn and used.

The point of the catechumenate, whether it enrolls adults or children, is to initiate Christians into the life of the community. Knowledge of the whole panoply of Catholic lore and practice, however, cannot be a prerequisite for the baptism of catechumens any more than it is for infants born into Catholic families. It was in reaction to lingering vestiges of gnosticism that Pope St. Pius X insisted on the obligation and *right* of small children to participate fully in the sacramental life of the church. The decree *Quam singulari* issued in 1910 stated, "A full and perfect knowledge of Christian doctrine is not necessary for first communion or for first confession." Later, of course, the child is expected "to learn gradually the entire catechism according to ability." In addition to correcting the notion that knowledge is the principal criterion of readiness for receiving the sacraments, *Quam singulari* implicitly acknowledged developmental stages according to a person's years.

Quam singulari set down two broad conditions for first communion:

> The knowledge of religion that is required in children in order to be properly prepared to receive first communion is such that they will understand according to their capacity those mysteries of faith that are necessary as a means of salvation and that they can distinguish between the bread of the eucharist and ordinary material bread, and thus they may receive holy communion with a devotion becoming their years.[6]

Any minimalist interpretation of *Quam singulari* that emphasizes only the child's ability to distinguish eucharistic bread from ordinary bread misses the intent of the decree. The child should be told about how the story of Jesus—his life, suffering, death and resurrection—is the core of the mystery of faith and the means of salvation. It is important that parents and catechists help children see holy communion as only one aspect of the eucharist. They should be told the story of the Lord's Supper and shown how the Mass is the memory of that event. They need not have heard the terms *unbloody sacrifice, transubstantiation* or *real presence,* but their attention should be called to the breaking of the bread, and they should be invited to share the body and blood of Christ with others who stand before the table of the Lord.

Are Children Full-Fledged Christians?

Catechumens—adults and children—would ideally receive the eucharist as part of the initiatory rites at the Easter Vigil when the story of salvation culminating in Christ's resurrection is told. Besides helping Christians associate the eucharist with the paschal mystery, this would be an annual reminder for the entire Christian community of what is celebrated at Mass.

It is not any different for a catechumen in the twentieth century than it was in Augustine's time. One hears the good news proclaimed and responds by committing oneself to following the example and teachings of Jesus. The doctrine that one must know is summed up in the creed, the Lord's Prayer and the twofold commandment, love of God and love of neighbor. Whatever else an individual learns, however erudite he or she becomes, the Christian should never lose sight of this basic outline. Faith, hope and charity is the substance. Everything else is secondary.

One finds support for this approach in an unexpected source. A century ago Horace Bushnell, author of the classic work *Christian Nurture,* argued persuasively that children must be welcomed as full-fledged members of the church. He felt that using a catechism to teach the very young child was ineffective. Better, he said, is the creed.

> It must be obvious that very small children are more likely to be worried and drummed into apathy by dogmatic catechisms than to get any profit from them. If exercised in them at all, it should be at a later period, when their intelligence is considerably advanced, that they may, at least, get some show of meaning in them to repay the labor of committing them to memory. [More would be accomplished if children] were trained, for example, to recite the Apostles' or the Nicene Creed. Here they do not merely memorize, but they assent and, what is more, do it by an act of practical homage or worship—a confession. And then what they assent to is no matter of opinion or speculative theology but a recitation of the supernatural facts of the gospel, taken simply as facts. For these facts are intelligible even to a very young child and will be recited always with the greater interest that the recitation is a religious act or confession.[7]

A further argument in favor of this approach is that the creed is a prayer of the Christian community as a whole. Children who are fully initiated recite it in unison with adults at the Sunday liturgy. Christians never become too advanced for the creed in the way they seem to outgrow the catechism.

Conclusion

One spends a lifetime unpacking the theology summarized in the baptismal creed, the Lord's Prayer and the twofold commandment of love. Although Augustine questioned whether any summary can better express in a few words what Christians are to believe, what they are to hope for and what they are to love, he also recognized that faith, hope and charity must be explained in many words as Christians grow in faith and wisdom. The presentation and acceptance of the symbol of faith is but the beginning. Catechesis cannot stop with these first steps. Catholic Christians never tire of reflecting on the *doctrines* of the church in order to come to a mature appreciation of its *doctrine* that is nothing other than the kerygma—the gospel message.

I acknowledged previously that lists of doctrines, medieval and modern, can serve a purpose. I also want to recognize the usefulness of "catechisms," especially the genre of adult catechisms. In the best tradition of the Council of Trent, adult catechisms move beyond basic teachings into a theological framework that is beyond the grasp of small children and most catechumens.

My complaint about catechisms is much the same as the criticism often heard of rococo architecture and music. In the sixteenth century, the Renaissance builders remodeled the ancient basilicas, introducing pilasters, baldachins and other ornamentation that obscured the simple, strong lines. The great Renaissance churches served a purpose not envisaged by the early Christians and even now have an attraction of their own, but they are far removed from the pristine spirit and function of liturgy. Similarly, catechisms serve a purpose: They present church teaching, incorporate information that is part of Catholic tradition and provide theological insights. But catechisms, like rococo art, too often obscure the basic structure of the baptismal creed—the work of the Father, Son and Spirit in creation, redemption and sanctification. That is the creed and doctrine that children need.

NOTES

1. Augustine of Hippo, *Enchiridion*. English translation in P. Schaff, ed., *Nicene and Post-Nicene Fathers (NPNF)* 3, 229–76.

2. Augustine of Hippo, *De fide et symbolo,* NPNF 3, 321.

3. Hugh of St. Victor, *"De quinque septenis seu septenariis," Patrologia Latina* 175, col. 405–14. According to the *New Catholic Encyclopedia* 7, Hugh's theology followed "the pattern of the historical economy of salvation, beginning with Adam's fall, culminating in Christ's advent and ending with the consummation of all things" (194).

4. Gerald O'Collins, *The Case against Dogma* (New York: Paulist Press, 1975), 5.

5. E. D. Hirsch, Jr., *Cultural Literacy* (New York: Vintage Books, 1988), 3.

6. The Latin text with an English translation of *Quam singulari* can be found in J. B. Collins, ed., *Catechetical Documents of Pope Pius X* (Paterson: St. Anthony Guild Press, 1946), 54–62, 158–65.

7. Horace Bushnell, *Christian Nurture* (New Haven: Yale University Press, 1967), 317–18.

CHAPTER
6

> "*Initiation of children is not about teaching cognitive religious truths. It is an event that remembers itself. What we are about in initiation is images, symbols and pictures of our faith: water, book, cross, oil, table, bread, people, candle, fire.*"

Initiation:
An Event That
Remembers Itself

RICHELLE PEARL-KOLLER

In this chapter I intend to describe how our parish implements "Christian Initiation of Children Who Have Reached Catechetical Age" and provide a rationale that underpins the choices we have made as a parish. What I offer here are simply a few examples of what one parish has done. In all of this I have been guided by the norms set forth in the Rite of Christian Initiation of Adults (RCIA). The catechumenate with children never can be separated from the adult catechumenate in a parish. I hope that through this report and rationale the reader will be able to reflect on both the "what" and the "why" of the initiation of children and draw some pastoral conclusions appropriate to her or his own situation.

My pastoral experience with the catechumenate with children is limited to children between the ages of 5 and 11. The rite itself seems to suggest that there are two categories of catechetical-age children: the younger children, between the ages of 7 and 9, and the older children, ages 10 to 18. "The process of initiation must be adapted . . . in proportion of their age" (RCIA, 253). Others (like Mary Collins and Don Neumann in this collection) address the initiation process of older children in ways that are appropriate to them, respecting both their growing independence and their psychological vulnerability. I speak only of the younger children around the age of 7 through 9.

When I think of initiating children into the Christian community, I am reminded of the writings of Black Elk, the holy man of the Oglala Sioux. As a young boy Black Elk experienced a vision that directed and carried him throughout his life. The vision was full of pictures of animals, people, winds, earth, the great hoop and circle. Later, as an old man speaking of that experience, Black Elk said:

> I am sure now that I was then too young to understand it all and that I only felt it. It was the pictures I remembered and the words that went with them; for nothing I have ever seen with my eyes was so clear and bright as what the vision showed me; and no words that I have ever heard with my ears were like the words I heard. I did not have to remember these things; *they remembered themselves all these years*. It was as I grew older that the meanings became clearer and clearer out of the pictures and even now I know that more was shown to me than I can tell.[1]

The reason I cite Black Elk is that I believe his words highlight so well what we are about in the initiation of children. Initiation of children is not about teaching cognitive religious truths. Initiation of children is an event that remembers itself. What we are about in initiation is images, symbols and pictures of our faith: water, book, cross, oil, table, bread, people, candle, fire. This became very clear to me 11 years ago when my own adopted Korean daughter was initiated at age 7. Because we lacked an adequate baptismal space for immersion, she was baptized by the pouring of water on her head. The bowl that was used for her baptism was huge and bright green.

A year later my daughter and I were at the Easter Vigil. As the bowl was being brought in at the water rite, my daughter shouted out, "Hey, Mom, that's my baptism bowl." As I looked at her that night I realized she had something that those of us baptized as infants do not have. She had a memory of her baptism. Her memory and imagination held that huge green bowl. Throughout her life she would grow to understand what the picture means. Black Elk's experience and my daughter's experience shape my catechumenal ministry with children.

Precatechumenate

The period of precatechumenate is for us predominantly a time of working with the parents of the children who are being presented for initiation. Usually these families have been inactive and disassociated from the church for one reason or another. When they return they are surprised to find that the church they left has changed. So, before even beginning to work with their unbaptized catechetical age child, we ask the parents to take all the time they need to become comfortable and at ease in returning to their own religious practice and worship. Usually we suggest that they wait about a year before enrolling their child for initiation.

During that year a variety of things may happen depending on the individual situation. The parents participate in our parish Welcome Program for New Members. They are given a sponsor who acquaints them with the parish. With their sponsor and other new members they participate in several small-group, faith-sharing sessions. At these gatherings participants share stories and explore the connections and meaning of faith, their lives and membership in a worshiping community. A catechist may be invited to work with the parents or, depending on the situation, they may join the Re-Membering Church group. Each person and household is dealt with individually. "Nothing can be settled a priori" (RCIA, 76). Throughout this time candidates are taking part in Sunday worship and the ongoing life of the parish.

Why all this time and emphasis on the parent(s) or guardian(s)? Because it is within the context of the parent's journey in the church that the child's journey takes place. The household is the domestic church for the child, the place in which the child is nurtured and traditioned in the Christian way of life. The RCIA states, "The children's progress in the formation they receive depends on the influence of their parents . . . and their example" (254). Thus it seems not only appropriate but imperative that the first step of the catechumenate with children focus on the parents. Writing of infant baptism, Mark Searle makes an observation that is applicable to the catechumenate:

> The liturgy of baptism depends for its ability to "translate" the child from outside to inside the church upon the reconstituting of that church in the liturgical assembly and particularly upon the reconstituting of the family in its organic unity as an *ecclesiola in ecclesia*. If the child is baptized in the faith of the church, then the identity of the family as constituted by faith, as itself a sacrament of faith, must be "confected" anew in the process and event of sacramental initiation.[2]

At the end of this period when the parents are ready and when there are, if possible, "a group of several children who are in the same situation" (RCIA, 255), the children are presented for the Rite of Acceptance into the Order of Catechumens. Though the RCIA states "this celebration is not normally combined with eucharist" (260), we do celebrate it at the Sunday eucharist. Throughout the whole initiatory process with children, we celebrate all major rites on Sunday. Our reason for doing so is that the purpose of initiation is to welcome the child into the Sunday assembly and bring the child to the table. To celebrate major catechumenal rituals apart from the Sunday eucharist appears to place a higher value on the comfort of the child, on intimacy and on privacy as more important than the tradition of the Sunday assembly. Further, the RCIA states, "Initiation takes place within the community of the faithful" (4). "At the celebrations the faithful should be present whenever possible and should take an active part" (9:2).

During the rite of acceptance, the parents are asked two questions: (1) What do you ask for your child? (2) Why do you ask this for your child at this time? The parents' testimony and the sharing of their story has such a profound effect on the assembly that it becomes a renewing event for the community.

Filling the children's imagination with our primary symbols begins strongly in this rite as the children are welcomed by the assembly, as they are signed from head to foot with the cross and as they are presented with the scriptures. Then they are dismissed with their catechist to reflect on the experience.

Catechumenate

During the period of catechumenate several things are happening with the children. The determining factor for what occurs is found in RCIA, 75. What we are about is leading children "to a profound sense of the mystery" (75:1). Children have a natural capacity to wonder, to get into mystery. All that is done in the catechumenal process needs to build on that sense. In the young children the ability to understand mystery is far deeper than their ability to articulate it. Throughout the catechumenate we need to trust the process of image making and to allow the word, the rite, the high seasons and feasts, the symbols, the prayer and the apostolic life of the parish to nurture, form and shape the children. As adults ministering to children in the catechumenate we have to let go of our need to control and measure the children's progress by means of verbal expressions and catechism answers. This being said, what do children do during the catechumenate?

First, they come to Sunday eucharist and participate in the children's celebration of the word with baptized peers and companions. There they chew the word at their level just as the adult catechumen would. Their catechesis is "to be solidly supported by celebrations of the word" (RCIA, 75:1).

In addition the young catechumens and their parents take part in parish liturgical events: Advent-wreath-making workshops and ceremonies; Christmas projects that provide gifts for the poor; and rituals of remembering and naming the dead. Experiences such as these "provide a catechesis accommodated to the liturgical year" (RCIA, 75). Along with their parents the young catechumens participate in the parish program, Loaves and Fishes. They collect food for a local food pantry and share in parish outreach projects to the poor and needy, especially in projects that connect children with other children. These activities familiarize the catechumens "with the Christian way of life and lead to . . . social consequences" (RCIA, 75:2). Through-out their catechesis children come to see that "the church's life is apostolic" (RCIA, 75:4) and that mission and service are central elements of the gospel.

Two other parts of the young children's catechesis are participation in our parish school or religious education programs when that is appropriate. Adaptations need to be made for individual cases. Young catechumens also join with parish children who are preparing to celebrate confirmation and first communion,[3] for "their initiation progresses gradually and within the supportive setting of this group of companions . . . children of the same age who are already baptized and are preparing for confirmation and eucharist" (RCIA, 254:1).

Finally, throughout this process the children have a special catechists who, with their families, serve as links to other families within the parish community. The role of these cate-chists is to help the children bond among themselves, to reflect with them on the catechumenal rituals after the dismissal and to provide special meetings that focus on experiences surrounding the basic symbols of initiation: water, oil, book, cross, table, bread.

In this style of catechesis children learn the Christian way of life by "doing it" and by watching their parents and other members of the assembly living in fidelity to the gospel. This kind of catechesis is comparable to an apprenticeship. It is the style of catechesis that fills the children's imagination with memories and images never to be forgotten, and with pictures whose meaning, as Black Elk said, will become clear over a person's lifetime.

Purification and Enlightenment

Now begins the period of final preparation for initiation. The church "on the basis of the testimony of parents, of catechists and of the children's reaffirmation of their intention . . . makes the election" (RCIA, 278). I am reminded of young Matthew who for several Sundays before the rite of election kept asking, "Dad is this the day of my baptism? Is it time yet?" Surely in the young child this is "reaffirmation of intent," as was his response to the question, "Do you want to be baptized and follow Jesus?" "Yes, please," he shouted to the assembly.

The rite of election can truly be an event that remembers itself. The children's names are called: "Matthew, Emily, Josiah," and they come forward to print their name in the Book of the Elect. I am always touched as I watch the children print their names. Printing takes so much coordination for young children. Inscribing their name is like searing their memory with the great effort needed to live the gospel of Jesus. Every Sunday when they return to church, there stands the huge Book of the Elect with their names visible to all. And they remember! Initiation is about events and processes that remember themselves.

On the third, fourth and fifth Sundays of Lent we celebrate the penitential rite (scrutinies) with great boldness, praying that these children will be sheltered and protected from the evil rampant in our society. Here we again turn for direction to the adult rite of scrutiny (RCIA, 141), which is so different from the scrutiny/penitential rite set forth for children. In the adult scrutiny, there is prayer for deliverance from sin in its most radical sense. Whereas the scrutiny provided for children (RCIA, 291–303) waters down this radical notion of sin in favor of a private, trivialized understanding, mixing first confession and evangelical scrutinies in one ceremony. Here, as in other instances of implementing the children's catechumenate, we would do well to look to the Rite of Infant Baptism, which, in its exorcism, certainly does not subjectivize or trivialize evil. The scrutiny is a time to cry out *"Kyrie,* be our ruler." "Triumph, Jesus Christ, over the power of darkness." "Be *Kyrios* in the lives and hearts of these children, shielding them from the influence of such sins as competitiveness, greed or sexism, which pervade our world."

Initiation

We initiate our children at the Easter Vigil, which begins at 8:00 PM with a huge bonfire in the parking lot. As we huddled in the darkness and the fire was lit this Holy Saturday, one of the children shouted, "Wow, it's like fireworks!" That's what it should be. "Like fireworks." Children remember fireworks. After the fire, the lighting of the candles and the readings, comes baptism. This year for the first time we had a baptismal pool large enough for immersion of our three young catechumens. They removed their sweat outfits and, garbed in shorts and T-shirts, got into the pool. Water was poured all over them. Lots of water. They shivered and shook. Then they emerged from the pool, dressed in white robes and received the anointing of confirmation with so much chrism that its fragrance filled the church. After confirmation the children processed through the church bringing Easter shalom to the assembly. Later they heard their names again as they were invited to the table, "Matthew, Emily, Josiah! See this bread! It is for you so that you will never be hungry again." I recalled Black Elk: "I never had to remember the pictures, they remembered themselves."

Mystagogy

The children who were initiated at the Easter Vigil take front seats in the assembly on the Sundays of Easter. At the Sunday eucharist they regularly attend, they are again formally welcomed to the table. Their catechist meets with them to talk about what happened. Their parents, too, gather to discuss the meaning of the experience for themselves and for their children.

Writing about their experience of the Easter Vigil, two children said, "That night my Mom read a story from the book. [Each child received a copy of Jean Vanier's *I Meet Jesus*[4] at the Easter Vigil.] I liked the story. The next morning I smelled the oil from baptism. And my mom did, too. It smelled good! [Imagine so much oil that its fragrance lingered through the night!] I liked the book. It is like the big book at church. The bread was good. Thank you."

Ritual here touches the imagination and the feelings. Entering the ritual the children are transformed and shaped at a deep level. Ritual enables the children to know the mystery even though they are unable to verbalize that understanding.

In implementing the catechumenate with children, we must trust the process and know that, if done well, the ritual and pictures *will remember themselves*. Living with us, coming to the table with us Sunday after Sunday, the children discover what it means to belong to a community of people who share a common story, a common bread and a common task in the world —to do justice and mercy. Truly, initiation remembers itself.

NOTES

1. John G. Neihardi, *Black Elk Speaks* (New York: Pocket Books, 1972), 41.

2. Mark Searle, "Infant Baptism Reconsidered" in *Alternative Futures for Worship 2: Baptism and Confirmation,* ed., Mark Searle (Collegeville: The Liturgical Press, 1987), 37.

3. For this preparation, we use Jean Vanier's *I Walk with Jesus* (New York: Paulist Press, 1986).

4. Jean Vanier, *I Meet Jesus* (New York: Paulist Press, 1982).

CHAPTER
7

"*Friendship will have times of harmony and times of conflict. Such is the nature of growth in the paschal way of life. The friendship will be marked with moments of the cross and moments of resurrection. That is the journey of faith.*"

Companions:
The Role of Peers

DON NEUMANN

Before discussing the role of companions in a catechumenate for children, some preliminary remarks about the context of the catechumenate for children in the Rite of Christian Initiation of Adults (RCIA) are needed. A presumption of "Christian Initiation of Children Who Have Reached Catechetical Age" is that everything from the first 251 paragraphs has been read and understood by those responsible. There is really only one catechumenate, embracing everyone from catechetical age to adulthood and answering the pastoral needs of all inquirers in each parish. Catechetical age children are under the same catechumenate formation process as adults (although adaptations are made according to the age and ability of the children). Only by understanding the adult order can one make responsible adaptations for children of catechetical age.

Because children are able to hear "the mystery of Christ proclaimed, consciously and freely seek the living God and enter the way of faith and conversion as the Holy Spirit opens their hearts," they can experience the joy of coming to faith as participants and responders to God's grace so freely offered (RCIA, 1). As with adults, children of catechetical age take a journey that is gradual, usually taking longer than the nine-month-school-year model of religious education. With rites and periods along the way to mark the growth of the children in faith, the catechumenate for children should take place in the midst of the community, which is actively involved in their formation and support. Companioning begins here as the basic responsibility of all the baptized. The whole parish is called to be companion, example, sister or brother to all who come to the church for faith. Without this foundational awareness the role of peer companion is always apt to be neglected. The purpose of the catechumenate, whether for children or adults, is to form persons in a life that is consistent with the life and teachings of Jesus Christ, so that they may make choices based on gospel values. This is best done by immersing inquirers and catechumens into the daily life of the community so that they can live as the community lives and see how the community puts its teachings into practice. What Tertullian said in the third century is still true today: "Christians are made, not born." Like anything well made, this takes time, concentration and love.

The Method: Socialization in a Paschal Character

As with adults, the catechumenate for children has a "markedly paschal character," shaping children in the wisdom and folly of the Lord's cross (RCIA, 8). Far more than classroom activity, paschal living is probably best learned in the larger arena of daily living and in the relationships and the tensions contained therein. Dealing with life's good times and hard times is a much more concrete formation in living the paschal mystery than a classroom can provide. Perhaps that is why so much time is spent in the Introduction to the RCIA on the first and most influential ministers of the catechumenate: fellow Christians themselves. The initiation of Christians is the responsibility of all the baptized. In particular:

> 1. During the period of evangelization and precatechumenate the faithful should remember that for the church and its members the supreme purpose of the apostolate is that Christ's message is made known to the world by word and deed and that his grace is communicated. They should therefore show themselves ready to

give the candidates evidence of the spirit of the Christian community and to welcome them into their homes, into personal conversation and into community gatherings.

2. At the celebrations belonging to the period of the catechumenate, the faithful should seek to be present whenever possible and should take an active part in the responses, prayers, singing and acclamations.

3. On the day of election, because it is a day of growth for the community, the faithful, when called upon, should be sure to give honest and carefully considered testimony about each of the catechumens.

4. During Lent, the period of purification and enlightenment, the faithful should take care to participate in the rites of the scrutinies and presentations and give the elect the example of their own renewal in the spirit of penance, faith and charity. At the Easter Vigil, they should attach great importance to renewing their own baptismal promises.

5. During the period immediately after baptism, the faithful should take part in the Masses for neophytes, that is, the Sunday Masses of the Easter season (see RCIA, 25), welcome the neophytes with open arms in charity and help them to feel more at home in the community of the baptized (RCIA. 9)

Great importance is placed on the ordinary day-to-day contact that the community has with catechumens. For children, the catechumenate will be significantly different from what it would be with adults because of parental roles, adult examples and the place of peers. But the goal of the catechumenate is still the same: to bring someone into the church.

Adults and children experience conversion differently. The conversion of children might be more aptly compared to "belonging," which is essentially a process of socialization and acculturation. It occurs more in the context of the dinner table than in a textbook. Belonging to a community is probably "caught" rather than taught. One catches it the same way one catches a spirit of excitement, adventure or sadness. One has to live close to people who are deeply enough infected with the spirit that enlivens the community. Before one knows it, the spirit is caught. Belonging is a learned behavior of a specific way of living acquired from ordinary good people who also have acquired it from their predecessors in the lineage of faith.

Therefore, the catechumenate for children greatly depends on forming and nurturing relationships with other believing Christians and building strong and enduring relationships that bear a "markedly paschal character." It will not always be easy. The church is not trying to establish an elite sort of social club of "conventionally acceptable" people. The church is real people in the midst of life's real problems and dilemmas, wrestling regularly with what it means to turn from sin and seek God. Into this community catechumens are initiated.

Being welcomed into the homes of parishioners and experiencing how they live their faith daily is how the formation of catechumens best takes place. Daily life reveals how faithful persons struggle to put into the practice the faith celebrated on Sundays, solemnities, high seasons and ordinary times of the church calendar. It is here, in ordinary life, that the mysteries of the faith receive their litmus test of authenticity. Perhaps that is why, for children, the process of coming to faith might be more beneficial if it centered on fostering relationships. Socialization and acculturation are not primarily intellectual; they take place by living close to people one loves and respects. While formal teaching is needed, the amount is less important than the social bonding that must occur, both at the beginning and throughout the process.

Companions and the Catechumenate for Children

The children's progress in the formation they receive depends on the help and example of their companions and on the influence of their parents. Both these factors therefore should be taken into account.

> 1. Because the children to be initiated often belong to a group of children of the same age who are already baptized and are preparing for confirmation and eucharist, their initiation progresses gradually and within the supportive setting of this group of companions.
>
> 2. It is hoped that the children will also receive as much help and example as possible from the parents, whose permission is required for the children to be initiated and to live the Christian

life. The period of initiation will also provide a good opportunity for the family to have contact with priests and catechists. (RCIA, 254)

A major emphasis in the opening paragraphs of "Christian Initiation of Children Who Have Reached Catechetical Age" is the strong influence placed on parents, guardians and companions in the process of coming to faith (RCIA, 252). Assimilation into groups of children of the same age who are already baptized and are preparing for confirmation and eucharist is presumed in the rite. This most likely will mean that children who are catechumens also will take part in at least some of the ordinary religious education in which their peers participate. In parishes with sacramental preparation programs that are separate from ordinary religious education programs, this may be easily achieved by inviting peers preparing for confirmation or eucharist to be part of the process of their sisters and brothers who are in the catechumenate. While the distinctions between the baptized and unbaptized must be acknowledged, much of the process of the catechumenate for children could be helpful for peers preparing for confirmation or eucharist. But to put catechumens into ordinary religious education programs that are not lectionary based, that are not centered on the liturgical year or that are not intimately linked with the rites of the catechumenate could do harm.

The purpose of peer grouping is to support a natural bonding of children of catechetical age so that they do not feel awkward and out of place as they journey to the faith and that they have peers with which to relate as they come to initiation. Peers support catechumens. Peer groups are not primarily to provide an easy way to "take care" of the religious formation of children who are not baptized. It is not the religious education program that must be preserved at all costs. It is the coming to faith that is crucial.

For this reason, existing religious education programs may not be appropriate for forming catechumens in the faith. This is the challenge for all who work in religious education. Many will have to reevaluate present practice regarding method, context and ultimate purpose of the programs we have in place.

Questions arise. Do our religious education programs use the best methods to form people in a paschal way of living, or are we just handing on warmed-over traditions divorced from daily living? Do the programs enlighten the daily experience of people to embrace the mystery of the cross (both paradox and contradiction), however it presents itself in their daily lives? Or are we still falling victim to the falsehood that "if you live a good life, bad things won't happen to you"? In truth, are we still offering "classes in Christian education," with a dash of gospel stories tossed in to be fashionable? Or are we offering a responsible biblical base for the major stories of faith contained in the three-year lectionary? Where is the reflection on the Sundays, feasts and seasons of the liturgical year? Where is the catechesis of rites (the signing with the cross, for example, as someone is accepted into the order of catechumens)? Who will ask about the connections between the Sunday eucharist and the way we live during the week? When will we again discover the riches of our rites as a primary source for learning what we believe?

Catechumens of intermediate and high school age may find that the parish youth ministry program can be the context within which this bonding occurs. For others it will be the peers they meet through religious education programs or through small base communities. Whatever fosters companionship among children who are catechumens and their peers should be natural, without pretense, and realistic.

Companions do not necessarily serve the same role as a sponsor in the adult catechumenate. The role of sponsor is defined as "persons who have known and assisted the candidates and stand as witnesses to the candidates' moral character, faith and intention" (RCIA, 10). *Guide for Sponsors* by Ron Lewinski (Chicago: Liturgy Training Publications, Revised Edition, 1987) elaborates on the role of sponsors as fourfold: representative of the church, witness for the catechumen, companion and model. Though all four of these images can be adapted to the role of peer companions for children, caution must be exercised. Respect for the natural ability of children to build relationships and for the role children play in the formation of each other's values and behavior is needed. Companionship that forms spontaneously is preferable to the arbitrary "assigning" of a companion with whom a child may have no natural affinity.

Elementary-Age Peer Companions

Children are not "mini-adults" and peers are not "mini-sponsors." There is not much potential for elementary-age companions to represent, witness, companion or model as a sponsor in a faith they have embraced for only a few more years than the catechumens. It takes years of grappling with life, baptism, sin and reconciliation to gain the wisdom necessary to be a good model of the faith. For younger children, a very simple style of companioning may be all that can be expected or desired. The function of companions in the catechumenate for elementary-age children is friendship rather than the traditional role attributed to sponsors in the adult initiation process.

Peer companions are needed because of the socialization process of the child in the church. With elementary-age children, what is often needed is simply pairing a companion with a catechumen and providing opportunities for them to become friends. Companions do not have to be spiritual "whiz kids" or exceptionally religious for that matter. They just have to be willing to be a companion to a peer on a journey of faith. On the journey, both will learn what it means to be faithful and what it means to make decisions on Christian values. Both will fall short at times, face up to sin, get up again and keep on growing. In doing so, both will learn what it means to follow Christ and live in a way that is faithful to him.

It is hoped that more than one child will want to be a companion to catechetical-age children who are being initiated into the faith. Nothing in the children's rite prescribes a one-to-one ratio of sponsors to candidates. Nothing limits this ministry to a few. Could a whole group sponsor one child? Or could one person sponsor several children? Confidence must be fostered in children to assume this important role. At the same time, companioning is also the fruit of the whole parish as it welcomes and nurtures those who come seeking God.

Adolescent Peer Companions

Having realistic expectations for peer companions is a requirement for both elementary-age and adolescent catechumens. Forcing adolescents to become adults too soon is not desirable! Every phase of life has its own purpose and function. Adolescence is a time of testing, questioning and maturing. It is not something accomplished in weeks or months. More often it takes years.

Realizing that the catechumenate experience may be two or more years in length, the role of the companion is to accompany the catechumen along the journey. For an adolescent this means growing in the faith with that catechumen. It is not enough for a peer companion to meet with the catechumen only at church or in the youth group. A peer companion and a catechumen should be available for each other in the ordinary ways at school and socially as well. In a relationship more similar to friendship than adult sponsoring, the adolescent peer companion can provide a crucial link in the process of becoming a Christian.

Like any relationship, this friendship will have times of harmony and times of conflict. Such is the nature of growth in the paschal way of life. The friendship will be marked with moments of the cross and moments of resurrection. That is the journey of faith. Any adolescent in a strong household of faith who is making a sincere effort to practice that faith could serve as a companion. Adolescent companions will reflect many of the same traits that the young catechumens are experiencing. They can share the questions that preoccupy adolescents as well as the search for answers. Simplistic solutions that were once satisfactory in childhood must be challenged. The tough part of the cross is the nonsense of it all. Only in this pondering is a Christian aged in wisdom.

Family-to-Family Companions

Perhaps even more supportive than matching peer companions to catechumens of catechetical age is the need to consider matching "companion families" to families with children who are catechumens. Because the celebration of Christian initiation is the "responsibility of all the baptized" (RCIA, 9), the involvement of whole families in ministering to families is a way to achieve the goal of inclusion.

The effect that families have on other families should never be underestimated. Children use someone else's parents as a rationale for how their own parents should make decisions on issues of concern to them. The attitudes, values and choices of one family may shape those of another family. Sometimes this dynamic results in actual lowering of standards and settling for mediocrity. But with families that stand out for their integrity and supportiveness with each other, unconditional acceptance and hospitality are hard to resist. Note how neighborhood children are attracted to them. People want to be like people who strive for a better life for others. If the same dynamic that motivates us to "keep up with the Joneses" were achievable in initiatory companioning, imagine how supportive and challenging one nurturing family could be for another family at this time in their lives. These peer companions can be the strongest.

For children, good peer companions can enhance the initiatory experience considerably. Children often agree with the song lyric: "I'll get by with a little help from my friends."

CHAPTER
8

"Inviting a young catechumen to join outreach ministries of the parish, such as feeding the homeless, assisting the elderly, visiting the sick, caring for the poor, exercising advocacy for the powerless, communicates to that boy or girl that being Christian involves a commitment to service."

Companions:
The Role of the
Adult Community

KATHY BROWN

According to the Rite of Christian Initiation of Adults (RCIA, 4), "The initiation of catechumens is a gradual process that takes place within the community of the faithful." This community, represented by the local church, "should understand and show by their concern that the initiation of adults [and children] is the responsibility of all the baptized" (RCIA, 9). This initiatory command is addressed to all members of the church, and in particular to the parish where there are catechumens. Members of the community of faith are the primary ministers to catechumens.

All parish members, whether children or adults, have a responsibility for the initiation of those who desire to become Catholic Christians. The question here is: What are the specific responsibilities of the adult community for the initiation of children of catechetical age?

The rite of Christian initiation of children who have reached catechetical age is generally understood to be for those seven and older. It also includes adolescents. This assumption is made throughout this chapter. It is important to state at the outset that the rite must be adapted continually to the individual whether child, adolescent or adult. Having said this, however, the responsibility of the community of the faithful remains somewhat constant even with the variables of age, personality and circumstance.

Becoming Christian

A discussion about the role of a particular person or group in the initiation process focuses on relationships. Many relationships are established with catechumens during the initiatory process. The young catechumens enter into special relationships with parents, sponsors, godparents, catechists, team, parish staff and entire community.

However valued, these relationships are not the end but the means toward a relationship with Jesus Christ. Children are initiated into a people in communion with each other but specifically in relationship with God in Jesus Christ. In relationship to Christ the community finds its identity. This relationship is formally established by the pouring of water, the anointing with oil, the laying on of hands, the thanksgiving over bread and wine. When children are initiated through these symbolic actions, they are immersed into Christ, becoming members of the body of Christ, the church.

At the heart of the church is the presence of Christ, made manifest in the community that gathers in his name. Theologian Kenan Osborne claims that "the church is the church only if and to the extent that it brings to presence Christ and his Spirit."[1] This presence is communicated by the members who gather to worship and to pray in Christ's name, who proclaim by their words and deeds the coming of the reign of God and the promise of salvation, and whose lives reflect the one they claim to follow, Jesus Christ. The salvific presence of Christ is freely given; the community responds by its faithfulness to the relationship.

The community's responsibility is to communicate the presence of Christ to children. Through the community's care with this task, children come to know and desire a relationship with Jesus Christ because they have encountered a faithful community. Consequently, the basic task of the members of a parish in the initiation of children is continually to point to Jesus Christ in all that they do and say. All other responsibilities of the adult community will find their starting point here with children.

Precatechumenate

Before children take the first step of initiation through the rite of acceptance into the order of catechumens, there are prerequisites. According to the rite they are to reflect "the beginnings of the spiritual life, the fundamentals of Christian teaching," "evidence of the first faith," "initial conversion," "an intention to change their lives and to enter into a relationship with God in Christ," "evidence of the first stirrings of repentance, a start in the practice of calling on God in prayer, a sense of the church, and some experience of the company and spirit of Christians" (RCIA, 42). These prerequisites for the inquirers spell out the tasks of the catechists, the team and the whole Christian community as well.

With the exception of knowledge of the fundamentals of Christian teaching, these prerequisites arise from experience. Even a knowledge of fundamentals must be reasonable, addressing the reality of Christian life. In actuality the prerequisites mirror some of the most important gospel values we embrace as Christians. Their significance must be demonstrated to the children if they are to be seen as worthy. This means that the adults must provide opportunities for these gospel values to unfold naturally in the life of the children.

But the responsibility of the adult community does not end there. Children develop a habit of calling on God in prayer when they witness the adult community at prayer. When the people of God give an example of repentance by their forgiveness of one another and by their participation in the sacrament of reconciliation, what is communicated is the value of forgiveness and reconciliation. The adult community has a responsibility to live what it proclaims as the way of Christians.

To live the way of the gospel is difficult not only for individuals but for an entire community attempting to be faithful disciples of Christ. Pope Paul VI wrote in 1975:

> It is often said nowadays that the present century thirsts for authenticity. Especially in regard to young people it is said that they have a horror of the artificial or false and that they are searching above all for truth and honesty.
>
> These "signs of the times" should find us vigilant. Either tacitly or aloud—but always forcefully—we are being asked: Do you really believe what you are proclaiming? Do you live what you believe? Do you really preach what you live?[2]

The authenticity of the adult community's witness reveals itself in living out the gospel in daily life. It is this authentic witness that attracts children to desire to become one with the company of Christians.

Essentially, the responsibility of the parish is to evangelize. Being a Christian witness is one of the significant ways a community evangelizes. The RCIA describes evangelization as the primary responsibility of the community during the initial period of the precatechumenate.

In *Evangelization in the Modern World,* quoted previously, Pope Paul goes on to say that "evangelizing is in fact the grace and vocation proper to the church, its deepest identity. It exists in order to evangelize." To evangelize is "to preach and teach, to be the channel of the gift of grace, to reconcile sinners with God,"[3] to celebrate the eucharist, to share what is believed and the reasons for our hope. In other words, to share faith with one another, to give witness by words and deeds of God's love, to invite others to discover the God of salvation, is to be an evangelizing church.

When one speaks of evangelization it is usually in an adult context. Many evangelizing efforts are directed toward adults. We must speak of how we can evangelize children as well.

Communities evangelize through actions that sincerely welcome children and that communicate respect and appreciation. Communities that welcome, accept and appreciate their children enable them to know that Christ is relevant for their lives.

A catechist assists children in connecting the stories of Jesus with their own experiences at home, at school, in peer relationships and with the larger community. The ambiguities, the sinfulness, the occasional experience of God's absence— these issues must be faced.

Through the development of constructive relationships with members of the parish, a child discovers the living God as one who extends a personal invitation to belong to the community of disciples of Jesus Christ.

So far we discussed what the adult community must do for the precatechumenal children. Before discussing the catechumenal period, we have to ask what the community must do for itself in order to fulfill its larger mission.

Clearly, it is in giving that we receive. This truth bears itself out in death and resurrection. In death we find life. But the human reality is that we, too, need to be fed, because we hunger for truth and for God's presence in our own lives. As Christ's frail human vessels, we stand in constant need of evangelization ourselves. We need to hear again the word of God proclaimed in a way that enlightens our lives. Our diligence in conducting liturgies with respect and our care in preaching gospel values that touch the lives of the people—all contribute to the ongoing nurture of the community.

Catechumenate

What has already been said about the responsibility of the parish for the precatechumenal children applies to every period of the catechumenal process. The necessity of witness and example by the adult community is always critical. But during the catechumenate, this basic ministry of witness is extended even further.

The text (RCIA, 75) states that during the catechumenate a catechumen is to receive a suitable catechesis, to become familiar with the Christian way of life, to be helped by means of suitable liturgical rites and to become involved in the apostolic life of the church. We discussed the need for the adult community to be witnesses of the Christian way of life. Let us look at other aspects of this fourfold process of initiation.

Catechesis, which is more formal during the catechumenate than it is during the precatechumenate, is, according to the RCIA, to be based on the liturgical year. Therefore, the assembly's habit of being faithful to the liturgical seasons, feasts, fasts and cycles of the church calendar influences the young catechumens. Children seeking initiation must be welcomed and included in these observances.

Celebrations of the word, adapted to the various ages of the catechumens, may be provided by the community. When planning and preparing for these celebrations and other liturgical experiences, young catechumens seek opportunities to contribute and participate. Through this participation adults communicate to them that their experience is of value to the whole community.

The adult community is also responsible for enabling a child to become involved in the apostolic ministry of the church. Inviting a young catechumen to join outreach ministries of the parish, such as feeding the homeless, assisting the elderly, visiting the sick, caring for the poor, exercising advocacy for the powerless, communicates to that boy or girl that being Christian involves a commitment of service. An adult community actively involved in apostolic ministries gives witness to the priority of serving all God's people.

At the end of the catechumenate it is the catechists, parents, sponsors, team and parish staff, in the name of the entire Christian community, who discern the readiness of the catechumen for initiation. Delay of initiation could, in the final analysis, be more of an indictment of the adult community than a judgment about the readiness of a catechumen.

Purification and Enlightenment

Besides being a community that witnesses to what it means to be possessed by the Lord, adults are invited to join the catechumens of the parish in Lent, the time for the period of purification and enlightenment. This 40-day retreat provides an opportunity for a parish to reflect on its Christian vocation. The adult community enters a time of repentance and preparation for the renewal of baptismal promises. Catechumens—children, adolescents, adults—join together with the larger community on the journey to Pascha. Several catechumenal rites celebrated in the midst of the community signal the final preparations of catechumens. Election, scrutinies, exorcisms, presentations of the Creed and the Lord's Prayer and the great Easter Vigil provide rich moments of celebration.

During Lent and Triduum, the adult community continues to provide the example of people on a journey. But catechumens are symbols, too. Through the lives of catechumens, the larger community is confronted again by the power of the gospel. Standing before that community, in need of prayer, are those who are struggling with the gospel, with being authentic witnesses, with their own frailty. The parish is to affirm them in their goodness, to strengthen them where they are weak and to walk with them through purification to enlightenment.

Mystagogy

For most children mystagogy continues for several years after initiation through continued education and immersion in the parish. The formal period of mystagogy takes place between the Easter Vigil and Pentecost.

A successful mystagogy has roots in the whole catechumenal process. The significance of the mystagogical experience emerges only when precatechumenal evangelization and the fourfold catechumenal formation are tended with care. Once again, it is the adult community that leads the way in this final period of initiation. Mystagogy is "a time for the community and the neophytes together to grow in deepening their grasp of the paschal mystery and in making it part of their lives through meditation on the gospel, sharing in the eucharist and doing works of charity" (RCIA, 244). Through liturgical celebrations and through the continuing care given by the adults, the young neophyte will begin the transition to full responsibility in the community of the faithful. By the adult example of discipleship of Jesus Christ, the newly initiated child will embrace the gospel and bring it to his or her own life.

The goal of the catechumenate for children is the discovery of the eucharist as a deed that gathers up all of life. Sponsors can assist by their example, by their word, by their love. But the whole parish must center around the eucharistic table. Veteran Catholics must be asked to talk with children or families becoming Catholic about this eucharistic center of faith. At the eucharistic table the child meets both the promise and the commitment of Christian initiation.

Parents

Unfortunately, the relationship that some children have with their parents can frustrate an understanding of God's love for them. Often it is parental apathy that stands in the way of a child's desire to join the Christian community. Other times it is the parents who have decided that their child will be baptized, no matter what! This is hardly inviting for a child who finds herself or himself dumped on the parish steps.

The importance of the parents in Christian initiation is clear. Before a child can be accepted into the order of catechumens, he or she must have parental permission (RCIA, 252). The hope is that the parents will want to join their child in initiation (or, for some parents, in returning to the church). If this is not possible but the parents give consent for the child to be initiated, then the parish community must develop relationships between the child and other adults who can be supportive throughout the initiation process. This kind of relationship is especially important between sponsor and child.

It is best when parents can be involved with the initiation of their children. The inclusion of the whole family provides the child with an environment for faith to grow. Parental involvement means more than just orientation sessions. Families ought to be invited to meet together to share the meaning of the word of God in their lives, to become involved in apostolic ministry and to pray together. In this way, the whole family participates in the formation.

The parents also could meet separately to share the word of God, to discover its relevance and message for their lives and to develop a relationship with other parents whose children are being initiated. Catechists and sponsors need to involve parents, to stay in touch with them, to discuss the rites with them, to assist them in getting to know other parishioners and, consequently, to help them discover the presence of Christ in the community.

Sponsors

Sponsors are the primary representatives of the parish. Their selection and training is key to the whole order of initiation.

The sponsor is to be a witness of what it means to be a follower of Jesus Christ. He or she also represents the catechumen to the community. The sponsor is a guide into the life of the parish. Through the sponsor's diligent attention to his or her candidate, a child will experience the welcome extended by the entire community.

It is important that the sponsor be willing to share faith honestly and appropriately. To be a sponsor who has all answers and no questions leaves a 14-year-old adolescent out in the cold. But a sponsor who shares both some questions and some answers can offer a more authentic witness of faith.

Team

We have looked at the responsibility of the adult community. The picture has been painted in broad strokes. It is the parish catechumenate team that has the responsibility of defining how the picture will be painted. The task of the team is to enable the larger community to assume its responsibility of initiation. There is really only one catechumenate in a parish. Within that one catechumenate there are people of different ages. Each age group may need to meet separately because the order of rites and periods of initiation is adapted to different circumstances.

The team must help each group of catechumens: children, adolescents, adults. The team plans opportunities for all parish catechumens to come together in celebration of the rites and for socializing. The people ought never have the experience of separate catechumenates in the parish.

The team enables, encourages and educates the members of the community regarding their initiatory responsibility. This requires good public relations with the parish organizations and the parish staff. It also means providing members of the parish with opportunities to be evangelized, to be renewed in their own journey and to be nourished by the word of God.

Primarily, the team must be a model of the Christian community for all catechumens in the parish. Especially in large parishes where a child may be overwhelmed by numbers, the team, catechists and sponsor become even more important examples of discipleship. They are for the child the mirror of God's presence.

Conclusion

We have emphasized the importance of the relationships between adults and children in the experience of initiation. We have looked at the necessity for the adult community to be an authentic example of what it means to be followers of Jesus Christ. The responsibility of the adult community emerges as an essential ingredient in each rite and period. We conclude that the community is key in initiation. As self-evident as this may seem, many parishes still are initiating children without any active involvement by the larger community.

The relationships developed between the children and parents, sponsor, team, catechists and ultimately the entire community are critical for the development of faith. The community of the faithful, who through their words and deeds pass on the living tradition, are the enfleshment of the Christ. Without this community an individual would not experience the living reality of God's invitation to belong to the disciples of Jesus Christ. In communion with each other we are the church. But we are the church only to the extent that we represent Christ to one another.

NOTES

1. Kenan Osborne, *The Christian Sacraments of Initiation* (New York: Paulist Press, 1987), 88.

2. Pope Paul VI, *Evangelization in the Modern World (Evangelii nuntiandi)* (Washington, D.C.: United States Catholic Conference, 1975), 57–58.

3. Ibid., 12.

CHAPTER
9

"*Catechesis of first penance is rooted in the catechumenal preparation for initiation. We have an opportunity for a protracted catechesis of penance that gradually leads a child into the moral life of faith.*"

First Penance and the Initiation Rites

LINDA L. GAUPIN

W ith the implementation of "Christian Initiation of Children Who Have Reached Catechetical Age," which is chapter 1 of Part II of the Rite of Christian Initiation of Adults (RCIA), the church makes clear its willingness to provide a varied practice of initiation. For children baptized as infants the sacramental order of initiation has followed this pattern: baptism, first penance, first communion, confirmation, all celebrated over a period of many years. Currently our unbaptized children of catechetical age are initiated into the church through baptism, confirmation and eucharist, celebrated at a single eucharistic event.

For those accustomed to the former pattern, the text on children's initiation raises many questions about the order of the initiatory sacraments. One of the predominant issues is confirmation. Another important concern, however, is the role of first penance in the restored order of baptism, confirmation and eucharist for unbaptized children of catechetical age.

On the one hand it seems obvious that just as an unbaptized adult would not receive penance before he or she is fully initiated at the Easter Vigil, neither would an unbaptized child of catechetical age. On the other hand catechists who lived through the famous first communion—first penance turmoil of the 1970s, may be confused about first penance in the restored order. The aim of this chapter is to provide some clarifications about first penance in light of the new order of initiation of children. First, we will explore the meaning of penance and reconciliation in light of our initiatory practices for unbaptized children of catechetical age. Second, we will attempt to provide some direction for a catechesis of first penance following sacramental initiation.

Penance, Reconciliation and Initiation

The text of the order of the Christian initiation of children provides an occasion for examining anew the first penance—first communion issues. The major contribution of the rite to this issue is that it provides a proper foundation for understanding the meaning of penance and reconciliation in Christian life for children. It takes us beyond the specific issue of order and situates the discussion within the more basic terms of the meaning of penance and reconciliation in light of Christian initiation.

In the celebration of the sacraments of initiation the unbaptized child of catechetical age receives baptism, confirmation and eucharist together. First penance does not take place until after the child has been fully initiated. This does not mean, however, that the realities of penance and reconciliation are omitted in the catechumenate.

The entire process of becoming a Christian is one of conversion: transformation into right relationships with God and incorporation into a reconciled community. "The mystery of reconciliation is, at the same time, the mystery of conversion."[1] Consequently throughout the process the unbaptized child of catechetical age is gradually led into the wonder of these mysteries in accord with her or his ability and growth in faith.

Baptism and eucharist, the primary and fundamental sacraments of reconciliation, mark the child's entrance into these realities. The celebration and all that has led up to it provide the foundation for the child's later catechesis of first penance after initiation. In his excellent article on penance and reconciliation, M. Francis Mannion states: "Christian baptism is the first and original sacrament of reconciliation and forgiveness of sin, not only in a temporal sense but in a primordial and paradigmatic one, and all other forms and concepts of reconciliation are subservient to and derivative of what is said of baptism."[2]

This sense is clearly substantiated in the Rite of Penance (RP). In the introduction we read: "This victory is *first* brought to light in baptism where our fallen nature is crucified with Christ so that the body of sin may be destroyed and we may no longer be slaves to sin but rise with Christ and live for God. . . . In the eucharist Christ is present and is offered as 'the sacrifice that has made our peace' with God and in order that 'we may be brought together in unity with the Holy Spirit'" (RP, 2). Thus initiation starts the continuing conversion that marks the life of discipleship, establishes union with Christ and provides that ecclesial experience needed for understanding penance and reconciliation. At the same time it is the foundation for the future catechesis of first penance after initiation.

The liturgical season of Lent offers a special opportunity to deepen the child's awareness of these realities. The rite accommodated for unbaptized children of catechetical age states that the election or enrollment of names marks the "beginning of the period of final preparation for the sacraments of initiation, during which the children will be encouraged to follow Christ with greater generosity" (RCIA, 277).

This catechumenal period contains the penitential rites (scrutinies) adapted for children. "These penitential rites, which mark the second step in the children's Christian initiation, are major occasions in their catechumenate. They are held within a celebration of the word of God as kind of a scrutiny, similar to the scrutinies in the adult rite. Thus the guidelines given for the adult rite (RCIA, 141–46) may be followed and adapted, since the children's penitential rites have a similar purpose." (RCIA, 291)

Catechists should carefully read the introductions as well as the rites themselves. A careless reading may leave the impression that the unbaptized child of catechetical age is to receive first penance before initiation. Although some may feel that celebrating the three sacraments of initiation before first penance is an exception, the recent history of the first penance—first communion debate may leave confusion about the nature of this rite.

This penitential rite is one of the more puzzling aspects of the order of Christian initiation of children.[3] First, it is difficult to ascertain for whom the rite is primarily directed. The introduction to the chapter for children states: "This form of the rite of Christian initiation is intended for children, not baptized as infants, who have attained the use of reason and are of catechetical age" (RCIA, 252). Consequently, is this penitential rite primarily for unbaptized children preparing for full initiation or is it for baptized children of the same age?

> Along with the children, their godparents and their baptized companions from the catechetical group participate in the celebration of these penitential rites. Therefore the rites are to be adapted in such a way that they also benefit the participants who are not catechumens. In particular, these penitential rites are a proper occasion for baptized children of the catechetical group to celebrate the sacrament of penance for the first time. When this is the case, care should be taken to include explanations, prayers, and ritual acts that relate to the celebration of the sacrament with these children. (RCIA, 293)

Second, the rite seems to parallel the penitential rite (scrutiny) for baptized but uncatechized adults who are preparing for confirmation and eucharist. The adult rite (RCIA, 459–61) is similar in content to the children's rite (RCIA, 291–93). The introduction to the penitential rite (scrutiny) for baptized but uncatechized adults (RCIA, 463) states that it is "solely for celebrations with baptized adults preparing for confirmation and eucharist or the reception into full communion of the Catholic church."

Considering the similarities, it seems that the penitential rite (scrutiny) for children is likewise appropriate for children who were baptized as infants but were not catechized or for children who were baptized in another Christian tradition and now are seeking reception into the full communion of the Catholic church.

The adaptation of the scrutinies for children is further substantiated if we examine the remainder of RCIA, 463, concerning the penitential rites for baptized adults:

> Because the prayer of exorcism in the three scrutinies for catechumens who have received the church's election properly belongs to the elect and uses numerous images referring to their approaching baptism, those scrutinies of the elect and this penitential rite for those preparing for confirmation and eucharist have been kept separate and distinct. Thus, no combined rite has been included in Appendix I.

Conversion and Reconciliation

The central issue here is: How can we best lead the unbaptized child of catechetical age more deeply into the mysteries of conversion and reconciliation as he or she prepares for full initiation into the church? In light of all that has been said previously on the role of conversion and reconciliation for the unbaptized child of catechetical age preparing for initiation, *the celebration of the three scrutinies would better strengthen a child's faith in the mysteries.* In RCIA, 143, the introduction to the adult rites of scrutiny, we read that through the celebration of the scrutinies the elect are gradually led into the mystery of sin, and their spirit is filled with Christ the redeemer so that from the first to the final scrutiny they should progress in their perception of sin and their desire for salvation.

Catechesis for children, accommodated to their age, ability and growth in faith, leads to and flows from the nature of these scrutinies, enabling the child to name and examine the things that have power over them and tempt them away from Christ in our society. The scrutinies have a twofold purpose. They are meant to *uncover* and *heal* all that is weak, defective and sinful in the heart of the elect (RCIA, 141). The first task of catechesis of the scrutinies, therefore, is to uncover what is weak and sinful in being a child in the world today. A child who seeks initiation into the church does so in a society that breeds hostility resulting in the exploitation and the rejection of children. "Exploitation and rejection, suffering and death, failure to show a clear path to identity and self-worth are as much a part of the cultural experience of our children as belonging and sharing and nurturance and affirmation."[4] Our children also come to us in a society where violence toward peers, patterns of precocious sexual behavior and pervasive permissiveness have become temptations that are commonplace. It is not easy to be a child today.

The second purpose of the catechesis of the scrutinies is to enable the children to see how the church provides healing, strength and support. In this context our unbaptized children of catechetical age need to know how the paschal mystery addresses this condition. They need to know how the mysteries of conversion and reconciliation touch their lives in a fundamental way. Catechesis and liturgical celebration of the scrutinies can enable children to explore the mysteries of conversion, reconciliation and God's loving mercy in their lives for the present and for the future.

The potential of the scrutinies should not be overlooked during the child's final preparation for initiation. They provide an opportunity for exploring the mysteries of redemption that will be foundational for the preparation for first penance following initiation.

Catechesis of First Penance

Catechesis of first penance is rooted in the catechumenal preparation for initiation. We have an opportunity for a protracted catechesis of penance that gradually leads a child into the moral life of faith. This catechesis includes moral formation and the ongoing conversion appropriate to members of the church at every level of individual and communal existence. This does not happen in a matter of weeks. It is part of the larger journey begun by the child long before initiation.

The fundamental question that must be addressed in this catechesis for first penance is: What is the meaning of penance and reconciliation in a postbaptismal context? Once again we are indebted to the work of Mannion who points out that the words "penance" and "reconciliation" lack stability in usage. In light of this, he offers some terminological stability for each word within a postbaptismal context.

Reconciliation "is the overcoming of the break with the community of believers, and with God, that takes place through a falling away from baptismal grace.[5]

Penance, on the other hand is a more inclusive term. It refers to the "comprehensive dynamic that involves the whole church, as well as the individual believer, in building up and ennobling corporate existence in Christ. It has to do with continual growth within the body of the church. It deals typically with ongoing conversion and moral transformation."[6]

This sense of penance is also presented in the apostolic exhortation of Pope John Paul in 1984: "If we link penance with the *metanoia* that the synoptics refer to, it means the inmost change of heart under the influence of the word of God and in the perspective of the reign of God. . . . It is one's whole existence that becomes penitential, that is to say, directed toward a continuous striving for what is better."[7]

The task of catechesis of first penance then is to lead the child gradually into the mysteries of penance and reconciliation within a postbaptismal context. The nature of this catechesis is rooted in that of the catechumenate. The catechumenate forms children and adults in the faith of the church by means of a paradigm that is different from the pedagogical paradigm used in religious education.[8] The catechumenal paradigm focuses on conversion therapy that emphasizes the word of God, spiritual growth, journey, community, liturgical sense and God's graciousness.

Thus the primary source of catechesis for first penance is Christian initiation. Just as a lectionary-based catechesis is the primary way to break open the great stories of salvation during the catechumenate, so, too, does the scriptural repertory in the RP provide the primary source of catechesis for breaking open the stories of penance and reconciliation. The issues of doctrine related to penance and reconciliation are raised through the scriptural repertory found in the rite of scrutiny, which also then sets the agenda and hands on our beliefs pertaining to penance and reconciliation within the Catholic Christian tradition.

Catechesis and Celebration

The celebration of the liturgical rites of initiation wedded to catechesis of first penance is crucial, just as it marked the catechumenal journey of the child. The nonsacramental penitential celebrations found in Appendix II of the RP may be used to mark the journey of the child before the sacramental reception of penance. The rite states that these celebrations "are beneficial in fostering the spirit and virtue of penance among individuals and communities; they also help in preparing a more fruitful celebration of the sacrament of penance" (RP, Appendix II, 1).

The themes of the penitential celebrations root the catechesis of first penance within the initiatory experience. These themes include the following:

— penance leads to a strengthening of baptismal grace;
— penance prepares for a fuller sharing in the paschal mystery of Christ for the salvation of the world;
— sin and conversion;
— the Beatitudes; and
— God comes to look for us.

The catechesis of first penance also should include the help and example of the child's companions (peer group), parents and other community members. Just as this communal context was essential in the catechumenate, so is it crucial for the catechesis of first penance for several reasons. First, it is probable that issues of penance and reconciliation have already arisen during the catechumenate of the child. They point to the child's need for the healing of the brokenness, of a fractured family, of crushed hopes or of the weakness of other individuals in the family.[9] The catechesis of first penance must address the needs of the family as well as that of the child. Second, the communal context reinforces not only what has gone on previously in the catechumenate but also the aspects of ennobling and building up the community that are essential to penance and reconciliation. Last, the child's progress in formation for first penance depends on the shared stories and the lived example of the community's experience of reconciliation.

The entire catechesis of first penance in the case of an unbaptized child of catechetical age builds on and flows from the entire initiation experience that has gradually led the child into the mysteries of conversion and reconciliation. The catechesis of first penance, following initiation, does not need to be telescoped or abbreviated. It does not have to be concerned with the boundaries of time so that it can be done before first eucharist yet separate and distinct from it. The catechesis of first penance enhances and expands the initiation journey out of which the child has emerged, familiar with the experience of gradual incorporation into community, of lectionary-based catechesis and of liturgical rites that mark conversion.

Conclusion

In this chapter we attempted to provide some clarifications and insights into the relationship of first penance to the restored sacramental order as found in the RCIA, 252–330. This rite provides us with a marvelous opportunity to enhance and enrich our catechesis of first penance with children. We hope to increase and restore appreciation of sacramental penance for our children and youth not only in the present but throughout their lives. We also suggest that RCIA, 252–330, provides a context for reexamining and discussing many of the issues that continue to rise in our practices of first penance with children baptized as infants.

NOTES

1. James Dallen, *The Reconciling Community: The Rite of Penance* (New York: Pueblo Publishing Company, 1986), 253.

2. M. Francis Mannion, "Penance and Reconciliation: A Systematic Analysis," *Worship* 60 (March 1986): 104.

3. A similar critique of the children's penitential rites can be found in Catherine Dooley, "Catechumenate for Children: Sharing the Gift of Faith," *The Living Light* 24 (June 1988): 309–14.

4. Mary Collins, "Is the Adult Church Ready for Liturgy with Young Children?" *The Sacred Play of Children* (New York: The Seabury Press, 1983), 6.

5. Mannion, 109.

6. Ibid.

7. John Paul II, "Apostolic Exhortation on Reconciliation and Penance," *Origins* 14 (1984): 435.

8. Steven Robich, "Christian Initiation of Children: No Longer a Class or a Grade Issue," *Catechumenate* 11 (January 1989): 10.

9. Don Neumann, "Caring for the *Anawim:* Catechetical Age Children," *Catechumenate* 10 (July 1988), 15–19. In this article, Neumann describes the opportunities to focus on reconciliation during the catechumenate.

CHAPTER
10

*"If we can accept children with mental retardation
as they are, an amazing thing happens:
We no longer see the disability. We see a child with
strengths and limitations, more like us than
different from us."*

People of the Heart: Initiating Children with Mental Retardation

GRACE HARDING

T here are many myths about children with mental retardation. Accompanying the myths are fears. People fear them because of misconceptions about their disability. Along with myths and fears goes the idea that because a child is labeled mentally retarded he or she does not have the ability to learn. This is simply untrue.

Introduction

In this chapter, I would like to explain some things about the condition called mental retardation in general and some things about the special children who have mental retardation. It is hoped that myths and fears will be dispelled and that readers will agree that these children are truly *people of the heart* and as such will naturally appreciate the heart-filled moments of the beautiful rites and periods of Christian initiation.

There are about 37 million adults and children in the United States who have some significant disability. Six million of these people have mental retardation, which makes this disability considerably important in our country. When we look at this condition, there are three things to keep in mind: degrees, acceptance, relationships.

Degrees. All disabilities occur in degrees, from the very slightest to the most severe.

> The term mental retardation, as commonly used today, embraces a heterogeneous population, ranging from totally dependent to nearly independent people. Mental retardation refers to a significantly subaverage general intellectual functioning existing concurrently with deficits in adaptive behavior and manifested during the developmental period.[1]

Mental retardation is often described in terms of intellectual function, as the following chart[2] indicates:

Term	*I.Q. range*
Mild mental retardation	50–55 to about 70
Moderate mental retardation	35–40 to 50–55
Severe mental retardation	20–25 to 35–40
Profound mental retardation	Below 20 or 25

Even though these degrees or levels of retardation look grim according to the definition, this data serves only the purpose of information. It may be helpful for readers to realize that a given person has various levels of abilities and cognitive strengths: some weak, some strong.

Acceptance. This is what any child or adult wants—acceptance for herself or himself in a group. If we can accept children with mental retardation as they are, an amazing thing happens: We no longer see the disability. We see a child with strengths and limitations, more like us than different from us.

Relationships. Once we have a relationship with a special child, myths and fears disappear and we discover the great gifts of love he or she has to share with us and with our church.

Spiritual Potential

All persons have the potential to be saints. Children with mental retardation are no exceptions. They have gifts that gently move them toward holiness and toward the Lord. However, they need, as we all do, good catechesis and a loving teacher. The gifts they share with a group are simple gifts.

Love. Most of these special children have a huge amount of love to give. They are not afraid to show their love for others or to mirror their joy at being in community. Sometimes this spontaneous affection frightens strangers. But this wonderfully human gift is a source of strength and comfort to many.

Hospitality. What an important Judeo-Christian value this is! How sad our Lord was when he did not receive the traditional kiss of welcome upon entering a house.

Children with mental retardation are usually most hospitable. They welcome others and offer their outstretched hand in greeting. They are curious to know *who* you are, not what you do or what degrees you hold. They wish to know you, the person, stripped of artificiality and any masks of adulthood.

Prayerfulness. When given the opportunity to know Jesus, these children radiate an attitude that is exemplary for everyone. Their childlike dependence on a loving God and their trust in the Lord brings inspiration to all.

These simple gifts, when they are nurtured in a loving environment, reflect not only the child's intrinsic makeup but also the gospel values we try so hard to embrace and emulate. These values are natural stepping stones to understanding and appreciating the Rite of Christian Initiation of Adults (RCIA).

The accepted method of preparing children for their life in the church has developed in a strongly cognitive direction over the past several centuries. When the world was younger we depended less on cognitive skills and more on affective skills for understanding faith. Storytelling, music, stained-glass windows and drama were used to introduce children to the faith. Gradually, we have come to depend on a less exciting form of learning through reading, writing and lecturing. Although these are good, effective tools, they may fall short of moving the heart and soul to inspiration and good deeds.

The catechumenate depends not only on the cognitive strengths but also on the affective, symbol-making strengths of the children to be formed into the faith. This is why the catechumenate is a fine vehicle for children with mental retardation.

Children and young people with this disability find new language difficult to comprehend. They need a sponsor to explain carefully and clearly what is happening. A sponsor can take nothing for granted and must take time to tell and retell the stories of faith. One young catechumen with mental retardation asked: Why do we stand and kneel so much? What do we celebrate at Christmas? What happens at Easter? Though other inquirers ask similar questions, a child with this disability needs a more carefully constructed answer.

If a catechist or sponsor looks at the learning strength of such children, he or she sees that they usually learn well on the intuitive, symbolic and affective levels. Their sense of intuition is uncanny. Special educators often have wondered how children with severe mental retardation can be keenly aware if someone does or does not like them. Pretense does not work. There can be no "phonies" around children with this disability!

When we catechize such children, we rely heavily on the use of symbols, particularly liturgical symbols. We take a liturgical symbol as it relates to a sacrament and create a lesson around a symbol. As catechists we try to clarify the way a symbol interlocks with a sacrament. We try to show how a symbol impacts on a sense.

The catechumenate is rich in symbol and rite. That is one reason why children with mental retardation can relate well to the entire order of rites and periods.

Period of Inquiry or Precatechumenate

As the gift of faith is awakened in the heart of these special children, they simply ask to belong to the church. The same questions about life and about Jesus will be there, but the questions will be more basic, more childlike. Adults working with children who have mental retardation may feel uncomfortable at first. A presbyter friend and I were talking with a young girl who wished to join the church. He spoke to her with such kindness and warmth. He carefully asked her questions about her background and her family. I was touched by his sensitivity. Afterward he said to me, "I'm out of my element with those young people." I think he was wrong. I saw him at his best, most compassionate self. He reached out to her with grace and assurance. He experienced, as all of us do who work with special children, that they bring out our best selves!

This period of evangelization and even the period of the catechumenate provide the church with the time to get to know the children with mental retardation who are seeking Christianity. Because there are no fixed times, the sponsor, the church and the pastor have opportunities to understand the way children with mental retardation conceptualize. In any catechetical session with these special children, the emphasis is placed on the human relationships that lead to the relationship with God. It is vital that a friendship occur in order for the child with this disability to feel comfortable and trusting of the sponsors and the church. As many authors have said, these are "storytelling times"—chances to share the stories of the gospel but also times to hear the stories of the child who will be received into the church. This nurturing will free both partners to share stories, ideas and hopes. Within this affirming relationship the seed of faith is free to flower.

Acceptance into the Order of Catechumens

Here is where the ritual beauty begins. Rites have a way of tugging at hearts. Ritual elements somehow touch the deepest part of human beings—without a lot of words. They do not "work" on the cognitive level but on the affective level.

Preparation for each rite is especially helpful for the child with disabilities. An actual practice session will imprint the importance of it upon her or his heart.

The language is important. Children with mental retardation will not be familiar with the words "rite" or "catechumen." Care must be taken to explain words that may cause confusion.

After a catechist discusses the rites with children who have mental retardation, they can be comfortable with the symbols and the flow. These moving liturgical experiences graphically speak to the heart and to the senses. Therefore, they will be intuited by such children. The more these special children are involved in the rite, the more effective it will be for them.

For children with mental retardation a rehearsal is appropriate for each rite. The unfamiliar can be alarming, whereas a bit of practice and a walk around the church where the rite will take place can help these special children to understand better what is to happen. In other words for children with mental retardation, the fewer surprises the better. The power and beauty of the rite seems to affect special children dramatically. Sometimes the family may fear misbehavior or misunderstanding, but when children with disabilities experience the holiness of the rite, they respond with faith and simplicity to entrance into God's family. It takes time to go over the actual rite, any questions, the prayers, the activities of the sponsor, the signing of the candidates.

During each rite there will be scripture readings. Although these probably will not be adapted for the specific needs of children with disabilities, the sponsor may take time before the rite to explain the meaning of the gospel passage to be read.

If a book of the gospels is to be given, children with mental retardation receive them also, even if their reading skills are not on a par with other children. They may be able to read on a lower level. The symbolic value of receiving one's own copy of the gospels *at church* from the presider can mean much to a child. It may be treasured and put in a place of honor at home.

Period of Catechumenate

All the components of catechesis are present during this period: community, message, service and worship. Because this is also an extended time of preparation, it would be wise to organize each of the four activities mentioned. The more sequential in development of thought, the more organized in planning, the better the message will be understood by the catechumen who has mental retardation.

During this period a brief overview of salvation history, an introduction to the life of Christ, catechesis on baptism, confirmation and eucharist, and some emphasis on the feasts and traditions of the church might be enough sharing. Too much information will be difficult for some children to absorb. Too much information confuses and frustrates. The rites between each period will actually be the most effective teaching tools for the children.

These rites place emphasis on the word of God. Even if a child's reading level is low, her or his level of comprehending the symbolism of the word may not be. Whatever rites are used in this or other periods of the catechumenate, children with mental retardation will appreciate the time a sponsor takes before the rite to explain and rehearse.

If a rite such as the anointing with oil is to be used, an explanation of the human uses of oil (healing, repairing, cooking, protecting) ties in with the holy uses of oil (anointing, strengthening, belonging). This shows the candidate that the human thing called oil is also a holy thing that sets people aside as God's holy ones.

In his ministry Jesus used ordinary things such as earth, water, wine, bread, oil and light to enlighten people about the reign of God. He showed the sacredness of all creation. Perhaps because these common things are raised to such high meaning, it makes it easier for human beings to own holy moments deep within their hearts—without words.

Election or Enrollment of Names

The significance of being called by name and of etching one's name in a holy book can be meaningful to the children. The more humanly they are involved in this rite the more it means to them. Having their godparents with them can make this a special and proud time. They are happy to share this experience with their godparents and glad to share their godparents with the community.

Period of Purification and Enlightenment

This is a time of more intense spiritual preparation, with emphasis on penance and conversion. Most children with mental retardation have already converted wholeheartedly to God by this time. They try sincerely to "be good," as they understand goodness, which is often a form of obedience, fidelity in prayer and kindness to others. They do not have the sophistication or mental ability to offend God seriously or reject God deliberately. Instead they will sincerely seek God and try according to their ability to be faithful and loving. Their sincerity and simplicity is bound to disarm and inspire their sponsors to a deeper appreciation of faith and of life.

Spontaneity is a better quality than intensity for this period. Too much intensity causes frustration, but a calm sponsor who gradually and spontaneously introduces a child to the love of Christ will succeed. For the catechesis of baptism, confirmation and eucharist, the words of Christ and the symbols used in each sacrament are reliable bases.

Guidelines for sacramental preparation for these children are probably available through most diocesan offices for religious education or divine worship. If not, Cardinal Joseph Bernardin of the archdiocese of Chicago has written *Access to the Sacraments of Initiation and Reconciliation for Developmentally Disabled Persons* (Spanish: *Acceso a los sacramentos de iniciación y reconciliación para personas inhabilitadas).* He tells children and adults with mental retardation, "By baptism and confirmation you have a place in the church that no one can ever take away from you."[3]

The evangelical scrutinies and presentations of the creed and Lord's Prayer during this period of purification and enlightenment are conducted in a way that causes no anxiety for the child. If the sponsor remains close to the child during this time and offers simple explanations of the rites, the creed and the Lord's Prayer, this should suffice. At times the sponsor almost becomes a translator of the language into simpler, more understandable words.

Sacraments of Initiation

The beauty of these sacramental moments will be in symbols that touch senses. And senses in turn inspire the heart. The words used will not be so meaningful to children with mental retardation as the symbols of the rites and the love of the community surrounding them.

The atmosphere of the sacred, the outreach of the community, the support of the sponsor, the entire ambience of the moment speaks for itself and captures the heart of the special candidate to move her or him into the experience of being embraced by God.

Period of Postbaptismal Catechesis or Mystagogy

This is a "forever time." This is a time when friendship and community prevails for these special young neophytes. In order for newly baptized children or young people with mental retardation to grow in appreciation of the paschal mystery they need community. Now the community needs to stand by them. Once members of the community reach out to these special children, they will not find it hard to stand by them; but as they continue their support and care, they will find that somehow the tables are turned, and these special neophytes teach the sponsors and others about Christ and strengthen their faith in him.

The entire experience of welcoming into the church a child or young person who has mental retardation can be enriching and moving for all involved. Our churches will be better for having this person with us. No child should ever be denied access to the church simply because he or she has mental retardation. For often it is this child who has the deepest understanding of God and the greatest appreciation of faith.

In 1978 the United States bishops wrote a pastoral letter on people with handicaps. In 1988 they passed a resolution to "reaffirm and recommit themselves to the guidelines, principles and practices" set forth in that letter. The 1988 resolution states: "We call upon the church leadership throughout the country to encourage conversion of mind and heart, so that all persons with disabilities may be invited to worship and to every level of service as full members of the body of Christ."[4]

NOTES

1. Herbert J. Grossman, M.D., ed., *Classification in Mental Retardation* (American Association on Mental Deficiency, 1983), 12.

2. Ibid., 13.

3. Joseph Bernardin, *Access to the Sacraments of Initiation and Reconciliation for Developmentally Disabled Persons* (Chicago: Liturgy Training Publications, 1985), iv.

4. National Conference of Catholic Bishops, *Resolutions* (Washington, D.C.: United States Catholic Conference, 1988).

CHAPTER
11

"*The Sunday liturgy and all the rites of initiation celebrate and form the faith of a child entering a Christian community long before and long after conversion takes place.*"

The Formative Nature of Liturgy: Cultic Life and the Initiation of Children

JOHN H. WESTERHOFF III

While the church has acknowledged the normative nature of adult baptism, typically the church baptizes infants. While the church has acknowledged that Christians are made and not born and has established a Rite of Christian Initiation of Adults (RCIA), little attention has been given to the Christian formation of baptized infants. While it would be an anomaly to refer to baptized Christians as catechumens, the fact that persons have been baptized does not absolve the church from the pastoral imperative to provide the type of catechesis with which the catechumenate was originally developed to address. This chapter addresses one aspect of the Christian initiation of children: the formative nature of liturgy. The Sunday liturgy and all the rites of initiation celebrate and form the faith of a child entering a Christian community long before and long after conversion takes place. A catechumenate team for children must understand the formative nature of liturgy in order to appreciate its full power to change an individual and the world.

Catechesis: Formation, Education, Instruction

There are three deliberate or intentional, systemic or interrelated, sustained or lifelong processes that are essential to Christian growth: formation, education and instruction.

Instruction helps persons to acquire knowledge and skills useful for responsible personal and communal Christian life in church and society. For example, through instructional processes persons acquire a knowledge of the content of scripture, the ability to comprehend and interpret its meaning for daily life and techniques such as meditation. Similarly, through instructional processes persons acquire a knowledge of Christian theology and ethics as well as the ability to think theologically and to make moral decisions. Instruction or technical learning *informs* but requires the ability to engage in rational processes of cognition that developmentally are not possible until early adolescence. As such, it is therefore neither a necessary nor appropriate activity for children or others who are unable to engage in formal operational cognitive processes; nevertheless, foundational knowledge such as the gospel narrative and basic skills such as oral prayer can be acquired by children through participation in formational activities.

Education helps persons to develop and actualize human potential and achieve individuation, makes possible the reformation of personal and communal faith and life, and enables persons to relate Christian faith to daily life and work. As such, Christian education is best understood as critical reflection on experience in the light of Christian faith and life. For example, through reflection on cultic life and other aspects of life within a community of Christian faith the church can reform its cultic life and thereby become a more faithful community. Education or humanizing learning *re-forms,* which requires a knowledge of Christian faith and life not possible until adolescence. Therefore, it also is neither a necessary nor appropriate activity for children; nevertheless, the process of reflection on experience can be acquired by children through participation in formational activities.

Christian formation, which inducts persons into the body of Christ, is intended to shape and sustain persons' faith or perception of all life, their lives, their character, their identity, their behavioral dispositions, their consciousness or attitudes and values. Formation is a natural activity known as enculturation, socialization about which we are intentional. Christian formation or nurture involves the experience of Christian faith and life, and, while it is a lifelong activity, it is especially necessary and appropriate for children. Too long have catechists placed emphasis on instruction of children while neglecting both the formation of children and the education of youth and adults.

Michael Polanyi, the philosopher, offered a comprehensive description of the scientific pursuit of truth. His genius led him to a careful analysis of the key roles played by what he called (1) apprenticeship and (2) the dynamics of discovery within the scientific enterprise. The first process, similar to formation or intentional enculturation, ensures that the next generation assimilates the established paradigms for approaching knowledge of the tradition and the character of living masters of the tradition through apprenticeships to these masters.

The second process, similar to what I have called education, ensures that these apprenticeships will not degenerate into a benevolent brainwashing but that they will aid new masters to dedicate their energies to revealing yet undiscovered truth.

The first process ensures a faithful binding to the tradition; the second ensures that the tradition will be kept alive through its renewal and reform. In the first process the master shapes or molds the apprentice into the mind, heart and behavior of the master; in the second the master frees the apprentice from captivity to himself or herself so that the apprentice can become a master.

Paul Tillich, the theologian, discussed similar conclusions concerning the Christian faith and life when he spoke of Catholic substance (traditioning) and Protestant principle (retraditioning). Tillich pointed out that they depended on each other for faithful life. He further distinguished between "inducting education" that transmits Catholic substance by processes that help the tradition shape the perceptions of persons, and "humanistic education" that supports Protestant principle by processes that help persons reshape the tradition. Furthermore, he contended that some educators placed their dominant concern on humanistic education and neglected a concern for inducting persons into a tradition. Even religious educators were more concerned about the development of the potential of the person than in inducting persons into the community.

Perhaps we can see this neglect of inducting education most vividly when we realize that typically we translate the Greek word *didaskalos* as "teacher" and *didaskein* as "to teach." The result is most graphic in our films of the life of Jesus. Typically, Jesus is represented as a teacher without a classroom traveling about delivering lectures in the form of homilies intended to convey beliefs and ethical principles. We seem to have forgotten that the same Greek words that we translated as "teacher" and "to teach" also can be translated as "master" and "to apprentice," that is, to live with or accompany, to observe and imitate, to be guided and shaped by life shared with the master. We must remember that we become Christian and acquire a Christian perception of life and our lives by apprenticing ourselves to a community of Christian faith.

The Formation of Children

Human beings are communal, that is, they live in social groups and share a culture or a set of common, learned understandings and ways of life. Foundational to culture is a worldview, an ethos or character, and a system of beliefs, attitudes and values. The means by which these are sustained and transmitted from generation to generation is known as enculturation, a natural process of learning through experience by participation in interactive processes such as communal rites.

In pluralistic cultures comprised of numerous subcultures the process of enculturation is complex and is typically accompanied by a process known as acculturation or the means by which persons are enabled to live productively in a second culture while maintaining their primary culture. For example, first-generation Italian immigrants may enculturate their children as Italians, but the children are also acculturated into United States culture. Of course, the opposite also can take place; that is, second generation Italian immigrants may enculturate their children into United States culture and acculturate them to be Italians. Nevertheless, in either case theirs is a primary or dominant and a secondary culture into which persons are inducted. Assimilation, on the other hand, is the process by which persons are inducted into a new culture through conversion, thereby leaving behind the first culture into which they had been enculturated. Biculturation is the process by which persons are inducted into a blend of two cultures. When this "melting pot" process occurs, persons are eventually unable to differentiate between them, and a new culture emerges.

Religion is an aspect of every culture. In a simple society where persons share a common culture, they also share a common religion. However, in a complex society where there is a pluralism of cultures and of religions, religion itself may become a subculture. For example, certain Japanese Americans can be Christians while other Japanese Americans can be Buddhists. As such they will have some things in common and some things not in common. Furthermore, Mexican Americans who are Christians may have more in common with Japanese-American Christians than Japanese-American Christians and Buddhists have in common. Religion, in this case, has an existence alongside other cultural expressions.

In such cultures religion as a cultural expression can assume various relationships to the culture. For example, some Christians may attempt to maintain their religious life over the culture by choosing to live in isolation. By doing so they may maintain their purity but at the expense of influence on the culture. Christians may also choose to participate in the culture. By so doing they may lose their distinctiveness or so identify with the culture that it is no longer possible for them to distinguish between being a United States citizen and a Christian. Others may attempt to maintain Christian faith and life but live in the culture so as to influence it; that is, they strive to be-in-the-world-but-not-of-it and thereby attempt to transform the culture. Those who choose this option strive to enculturate their children as Christians and acculturate them to be United States citizens. Of course, the problem is that the dominant culture might win and their children become enculturated as United States citizens and acculturated as citizens of the institutional church. There are also those who in adulthood give up the culture and/or the religion into which they had been enculturated and become assimilated through conversion into Christian faith and life. This is the function of the catechumenate generally.

However, to complicate the enculturation process further, there is an ecology of contexts in which enculturation takes place: the home and family, the peer group, the neighborhood, the day-care center and school, the church or religious community and the mass media, to name a few. When these contexts share a common culture and religion, it is easier to maintain cultural identity and purity of faith than when they do not. Mixed marriages, mobility, diverse peer groups, mixed neighborhoods, public schools and mass media each contribute to the breakdown of the enculturation processes within subcultures and religious traditions.

Formation is an intentional process of enculturation for children within a Christian community and a process of assimilation for adults who are entering the Christian community for the first time. In the first, formation is nurture; in the second, it is both nurture and conversion.

It is important to remember that Christianity is not essentially a matter of affirming particular ideas, of experiencing particular emotions or of performing particular pious acts. Christianity is a way of life based on a particular perception. Christian faith and life, therefore, cannot be acquired through instruction or education but only through formation. Education is necessary to aid us in being intentional and faithful in our efforts at formation, and instruction can provide us with the knowledge and skills needed to engage faithfully in critical reflection. Thus all three intentional processes are necessary for a faithful catechesis. However, in a complex society with a pluralistic culture, Christian formation is of particular importance. Unless formation is a high priority, we can end up with knowledgeable, skilled, educated persons who are not Christian.

Cultic Life and Christian Formation

While formation involves all intentional experiences within a Christian community, cultic life is of the greatest significance. Cultic life is a community's religious rites and liturgies.

In 1925, Willard Sperry, the dean of the Harvard Divinity School and campus minister for Harvard University, wrote *Reality in Worship.* In a chapter entitled "The Occasion and Intention of Public Worship," he suggested that the church shares with many other institutions common tasks that are religious in nature and that many of these activities are better done by institutions other than the church. However, he contended, the one unique contribution of the church is its cultic life. While the work of the church is real and intelligible through the life and actions of its members, whenever and wherever people meet together avowedly to address themselves to the act of liturgy, there the church is clearly defined. Liturgy is the original and distinctive task, the primary responsibility of the church. Everything else may be conceded, compromised, shared and even relinquished. However, so long as the church invites people to worship God and provides a credible vehicle for liturgy, it need not question its place, mission and influence in the world. If it loses faith in liturgy, is thoughtless in the ordering of liturgy or careless in the conduct of liturgy, it need not look elsewhere to find vitality: It is dead at its heart.

Our cultic life refers to all communal rites or repetitive, symbolic, social acts (ceremonial acts, prescribed behaviors and ritual acts or words) that express the sacred narrative of the community and its implied faith. These liturgies include rites of intensification that follow the calendar (once a week, month, year) and that shape, sustain and enhance the community's faith as well as increase group solidarity, rites of passage that follow the life cycle and promote meaningful passage for persons and the community from one state of life to another; and rites of initiation that induct persons into a community.

Within secular culture there are numerous rites that are intended to shape the community's worldview and value system. They, too, are repetitive, symbolic actions expressive of the community's ways. The dominant secular rites are spectator sports intended to support individualism (baseball is popular, and in such team-oriented sports we give a most valuable player award), aggression (the most popular sports are the most violent), competition (ties are considered unsatisfactory; someone needs to win) and cooperation, but the kind that supports nationalism (singing the national anthem, cooperating with your team in order to beat the other team). Advertising is a form of cultural rite that supports an economic system based on self-interest and consumption. These rites and others constantly attempt to enculturate us to particular ways that explain why, when persons entered the catechumenate in the early church to be formed as Christians, they were no longer permitted to attend public spectator sports. If we are to be formed as Christians, we must take our Christian rites seriously. This means making participation in the church's liturgies the heart of formation.

The question is: Why? Objective knowledge is important but secondary to personal adherence. Information about the Christian tradition is important but secondary to the incorporation of persons into that tradition. Consider that the meaning of the sacraments does not depend on reason or understanding. Their purpose is to make possible an experience of the reality of God's presence. Only later, after participation, can we reflect on that experience, name it, describe it and seek to explain its meaning for our lives. Just as we do not delay in giving children a bath until they understand hygiene or delay giving them their first meal until they understand nutrition, it makes no sense to keep children from the liturgy or prevent them from participating in the sacraments until they understand liturgies.

Our rites are religious by nature because they are revelatory of God. They participate in the natural flow of God's communication. Our doctrine is derived from participation in our rites. *Lex orandi, lex credendi*: The rule of prayer is the norm of belief. Liturgy forms community experientially. The essential nature of rites is cosmic dance (religion is always danced before it is believed), an entrance into and celebration of a meaning that is beyond definition and concepts, when only the evocative language of gesture and movement, color, sound and fragrance as expressed in art, poetry, music and repetitious symbolic gestures has meaning. At the center of all religion are symbols, myths and rites. Myths (symbolic stories or sacred narratives that point beyond themselves and reveal truth otherwise hidden) are not to be explained but to be performed through rites. Participation in the rite creates meaning that otherwise cannot be communicated. We can never explain our rites; rather, they explain us. Symbols, symbolic narratives and symbolic acts are the keys to a pedagogy of faith, to Christian formation. Christian faith is ecclesial and communal by nature. Persons embrace the faith not through learning doctrine but by participating in a liturgical community that symbolically shares and celebrates its sacred narrative.

Clifford Gertz, the anthropologist, asserts that religious communities provide comprehensive interpretive worldviews and value systems, embodied in symbols, myths and rituals that structure experience and shape understanding. As such, religious communities are defined as intentional communities that attempt to shape the subjectivity of persons so that they can feel, think and behave within a particular tradition and so can interact with others who do not share their understanding.

Unless our identity is shaped by our primary community through liturgical participation, we cannot live meaningfully in an open society. To put it in other words, Christians must be intentionally enculturated (formed) into the faith of the Christian community, even as they are acculturated for life in secular culture: They must learn how to remain true to their Christian faith and life and still function adequately as United States citizens. An ever-present fear is that unless the formative nature of liturgy is taken seriously, persons will be assimilated into the society, which means the loss of their sense of identity as believers in Jesus Christ and members of his church. H. Cantwell Smith explained it this way: A person may continue to be "a Christian," affiliated with the institutional church, but no longer be "Christian," that is, live a life informed by a particular perception. To be Christian requires formation in an identity-conscious liturgical community of faith.

Liturgy remains the key to formation. Ritual shapes our lives. To apprentice ourselves to the church as the body of Christ is to participate in its liturgies, its symbolic actions. John Austin, the English philosopher, in his book *How to Do Things with Words,* explains how the primary function of language is not so much to say something as to do something. We humans perform actions through our words: We promise, pledge, apologize, forgive, judge, rebuke. As a result, the words we speak cause effects in us and others; they alter relationships. Austin goes on to suggest that the most significant word-acts we perform are those that are ritualized, for they not only express us, they shape us. Liturgical speech is performative; it is deemed effective in that it does what it says: "I baptize you," "I absolve you." Furthermore, he points out, that we participate in these word-acts primarily to submit ourselves to their discipline so that we might become disciples.

Liturgical word-acts carry meaning prior to our understanding of them. They are significant because they make present a reality that we have not fully appropriated and that we appropriate only insofar as our participation in the activity itself shapes us.

We humans make rites and our rites make us. No community exists without a shared story and shared repetitive symbolic actions. Our ways are invariably objectified in ceremonial observance. Faith and rite, then, cannot be separated. That explains why, when the prophets sensed that the people had forsaken their faith, they attacked their rites as empty substitutes. But when the people had lost their faith, the prophets called them to return to their rites. Without rites we lack a means for establishing purposeful identity; we are devoid of any significant way to sustain and transmit our understanding.

In recent years social scientists have explored the significance of rites in the lives of human beings. As a result, some have gone so far as to identify human beings as liturgical persons, explaining that it is by their rites that you know who people are, how they perceive reality and why they behave as they do. Through their investigations of the internal structures of meaning and the significance of symbolic processes, they have concluded that rites, as symbolic actions expressive of a community's sacred narratives, are the primary actions through which human beings construct, transmit and sustain their particular views and values. Thus, participation in communal iconic symbols (acts, words, things) influences both experience and the interpretation of experience.

Still, the significance of rites in the formation of authentic Christian faith can be questioned. Calvin attacked rites as idolatrous acts; Freud contended they represented infantile eroticism; and Frazer saw them as primitive magic. Of course, rites can become all that. Rites can be used as ends rather than means. They can manipulate and cause great harm.

But it is not necessary for rites to exemplify these negative characteristics. Rites can be healthy. Indeed, when the church neglects its rites, it both loses an opportunity to shape the faith of persons and encourages their participation in other rites, such as public athletic events. In turn these rites shape their worldview and value system, leaving the church without influence in the lives of its people and without witness in the world. To neglect cultic life is to ignore the most important element in the formation of personal faith.

Through liturgy the church becomes itself, becomes conscious of itself and confesses itself as a distinctive entity. Cult is not a marginal or discretionary element in the life of the church. Through its cultic life the church is manifest as a community of faith. Indeed, through its cultic life the church maintains and transmits its faith.

The primary responsibility of the church is to be the church; it is the church most fully when it baptizes and celebrates eucharist. Through these actions, it transmits its faith and shapes its people's perceptions.

Cultic Life and the Christian Initiation of Children

Because liturgy is at the center of our church life, we humans are *homo adorans,* worshiping beings. Worship is the particular vocation of all Christians. No Christian is to be barred from liturgy; no baptized child is to be excommunicated from the church; children belong at liturgy. Children, if they are to be formed as Christians, must fully participate in our liturgies.

Children are also important to liturgy. Children know best the nature and character of rites. Children are ritualistic. Every parent knows how children love to hear a story told over and over again. Parents know how difficult it is to shorten a story at bedtime in order to get a child to sleep. Furthermore, parents know how important repetitive symbolic actions are to children even when they appear not to participate.

If children find the liturgy meaningless, perhaps we should examine how well we do the liturgy rather than make the child sit silently or leave. Children are especially suited to the vocation of liturgy. They have a natural sense of trust. They are open to the mystery of nature. They learn through play. They are imaginative and creative. They love the arts and are natural artists. They approach the world intuitively.

A healthy understanding of religion and human life requires an avowedly bicameral mind. There are two interdependent ways of knowing, two interdependent modes of thinking, two interdependent dimensions of consciousness. One is an intellectual way of knowing and thinking. The other is an intuitive way of knowing and thinking. It is the artificial separation of these two modes of consciousness—the depreciation of the conceptual and analytical aspects of life or the benign neglect of the symbolic, mythical, imaginative and emotive aspects of life—that has contributed to our present religious situation in the Western church. A truly religious person has developed fully both modes of consciousness and has learned to integrate their functions.

While healthy religion has an essential rational component, we must be aware that the essential core of Christianity—the experience of God—is in danger of being lost under a cloud of rationalizing. At the heart of Christian faith is a nonrational element that cannot be conceptualized or turned into discursive speech, though it can and must be communicated. To paraphrase Amos Wilder in his book *Theopoetic,* imagination is a necessary component of all profound knowing and celebration; all remembering, realizing and anticipating; all faith, hope and love. When imagination fails, doctrines become ossified, witness and proclamation wooden, doxologies and litanies empty, consolation hollow and ethics legalistic.

An overemphasis on the intellectual mode of consciousness has contributed to the demise of the intuitional mode and contributed to a sickness in the life of the church. It is the significance of the world of symbol, myth and ritual that must be recaptured in our day.

We must be careful, therefore, that our cultic life is not dominated by the discursive, the rationalistic, the didactic and the prosaic. Good liturgy focuses primarily on the symbolic. This is not to defend a shallow aestheticism or emotionalism, but to suggest that our rites are often characterized by too much discussion, talk, stereotyped actions, mundane music, unimaginative drama, nonexistent dance and naturalistic art. Parenthetically, when worship is dominated by the arts and celebration, children are at home, can fully participate and are nurtured as Christians. Furthermore, the church is a body of many members. Each, St. Paul reminds us, has gifts for building the body. Children have theirs, and it lies in cultic life.

Liturgy understood as celebration is, as we have said, at the heart of the formation process. By participating in the church's celebrations, our faith, our character, our consciousness, our experience of life in relationship to God and our sense of community are all shaped. Therefore, children's most basic need is to participate in the church's liturgies. No program of instruction or education can contribute as much to their formation in Christian faith and life.

Remember that Jesus singled out the spirit of childlikeness as a mark of spiritual maturity best communicated to us by children. The church as domestic family was the image Jesus presented when he included children in his coming reign. Children engage in liturgy naturally and can teach the rest of us about cultic life; more importantly, if they are to be formed as Christians, they need to be integrated into the faith and life of the church through the formative processes of liturgy.

Conclusion

If we are concerned about our children and their Christian faith, we must turn our attention to the formative nature of liturgy. For those who have ignored formation and focused their attention on the instruction of children, this may mean a radical change. It may mean a reformation in the church's cultic life, both to include children and to express more faithfully Christian faith and life. The thesis of this chapter is simply that we have no choice if we are to fulfill our vocation.

CHAPTER
12

"Children take away from ritual more than they are able to say. . . . Their openness to religious experience is greater than even their awareness or focused attention would suggest."

Children's Ritual Enculturation

PAUL J. PHILIBERT

The unparalleled success of the catechumenate during the past 15 years has given the American church new hope for authenticity but has also raised some new problems. Among these problems is the question of how to integrate the children of adult catechumens into the catechumenal community and the even broader problem of how to approach the catechesis of children within a framework of ritual enculturation.

Enculturation is the conditioning or modification of a person or persons according to an established norm of behavior. By ritual enculturation I mean the whole, harmonious order—the ritual ecology—of catechumenal rites and periods through which people change. Neither term, "enculturation" nor "ecology" is found in dictionaries before about 1975. Could that be significant?

The term "ecology" suggests the delicate relationship between all the elements of a balanced planetary environment: ocean, land, trees, air, life. Here, ritual ecology designates the relation between the way we think, the way we behave and the way we make symbols. If we talk about a person's awareness, we must also talk about that person's thoughts and actions. They are all part of a whole.

The ritual ecology of the catechumenate teaches in the context of sacramental action and enacts sacramentally what a community has learned in shared symbolic moments: rites and periods. Learning and symbol making go together. If this ritual ecology works for adult initiation, should it be normative for children's initiation as well? Clearly some people believe so.

My task here is to describe typical transitions in symbolic development to help answer that question. As children's understandings of symbols change, so does their openness to the church's call to conversion. Between the ages of 6 and 16, children negotiate conversion in a variety of ways. But, as we shall see, conversion is not always a clear, self-awareness process of conscious integration of teachings and social meanings. Much of childhood conversion—or better, *preludes* to conversion —happens by a kind of overflow of values and attitudes from the moral agenda of parents and other care givers. We have long known that this happens. But for a few decades we placed so much stock in logical development that we failed to appreciate the decisive function of many prelogical (dreams, symbols, common sense, the way things are) developmental factors. I am especially concerned to give full weight to these prelogical dynamics. No matter how fully developed reason (logic, rationality) becomes, it can act only on the symbolic content that experience and imagination make available for reflection. This content is acquired largely through prelogical processes.

In discussing how children develop in ritual understanding, three areas need attention: First, the rites of initiation ask the question *what* is the vehicle of ritual enculturation? Second, the development of rationality asks *how* children see and understand the rites. And third, children's motivation to participate asks *why* involvement in ritual at all? After addressing each of these questions, I will attempt to summarize in closing remarks some typical tasks for the catechesis of children in a ritual ecology.

What Are the Rites, What Happens in Them?

It would be unreal to proceed in a discussion of sacramental and ecclesial catechesis without addressing the painful ambiguity of the American parish's "business as usual." Our rites are in disarray, especially our most important (if also most familiar) one: the Mass. Typically we find thin, eclectic, uncoordinated elements being hauled together to "bring life" to the age-old rite of the Christian eucharist. Annie Dillard, a remarkably acute poet-observer, evokes in her book *Teaching a Stone to Talk* many typical problems parishes face:

> It is the second Sunday in Advent. For a year I have been attending Mass at this Catholic church. Every Sunday for a year I have run away from home and joined the circus as a dancing bear. . . . Today we were restless; we kept dropping onto our forepaws.
>
> No one, least of all the organist, could find the opening hymn. Then no one knew it. Then no one could sing anyway. There was no sermon, only announcements. The priest proudly introduced the rascally acolyte who was going to light the two Advent candles. As we all could plainly see, the rascally acolyte had already lighted them.
>
> During the long intercessory prayer, the priest always reads "intentions" from the parishioners. . . . "For a baby safely delivered on November 20th," the priest intoned, "we pray to the Lord." We all responded, "Lord, hear our prayer." Suddenly the priest broke in and confided to our bowed heads, "That's the baby we've been praying for for the past two months! The woman just kept getting more and more pregnant!"
>
> During communion, the priest handed me a wafer which proved to be stuck to five other wafers. I waited while he tore the clump into rags of wafers, resisting the impulse to help. Directly to my left, all through communion, a woman was banging out the theme from *The Sound of Music* on a piano.[1]

In olden times, Catholics had the uniform ritual action of the Latin Mass. It was often disgracefully performed, but almost always the rite unwound in an aura of mystical detachment. We never had to worry about wisecracks or smart asides delivered by the presiding celebrant in Latin. We didn't realize then the premium on order and predictability.

For 25 years we have been in quest of ritual relevance. There have been pragmatic consequences. We have dismissed or ignored what seems too difficult—the periods of reflective silence after readings or after communion, for example. Few celebrants have manifested an aesthetic or anthropological grasp of the foundational symbols of our worship tradition. The altar could as well be a stage prop for an improvisational actor as the *axis mundi*: the holy spot where heaven and earth meet in time and space.[2] The use of candles and other sources of light appears to be purely functional or rubrical, in no way seriously suggestive of the mystery of revelation that is purported to be taking place in our midst. Movements around the sanctuary are matter of fact and haphazard, unrelated to any sense that these actions are enacted in obedience to God's Spirit moving us to respond in prayer and action.

Commonly today's presiders attempt to laminate some-thing "interesting" over the apparently boring repetition of overly familiar rites. Annie Dillard again:

> The Mass has been building to this point, to the solemn saying of those few hushed phrases known as the Sanctus. . . . Now, as usual, we will, in the stillest voice, stunned, repeat why it is that we have come:
>
>> Holy, holy, holy Lord,
>> God of power and might,
>> heaven and earth are full of your glory . . .
>
> Now, just as we are dissolved in our privacy and about to utter the words of the Sanctus, the lead singer of the [folk group called] Wildflowers bursts onstage from the wings. I raise my head. He is taking enormous, enthusiastic strides and pumping his guitar's neck up and down. . . . The lead singer smiles disarmingly. There is a new arrangement. . . . The words are altered a bit to fit the strong upbeat rhythm:
>
>> Heaven and earth
>> (Heaven and earth earth earth earth earth)
>> Are full (full full full)
>> of your glory . . .[3]

I am more aware than Annie Dillard of the good news hidden in her horror story. Unlike her, I am a cradle Catholic, not a Quaker looking for signals of transcendence. I acknowledge the rightness of celebration marked with the style of a present moment of culture and the theological centrality of the communal action of a people. (Dillard's essay, from which I extract only snatches here, is in fact quite sophisticated in its grasp of Catholic theology when seen in her own remarkable context.) But despite the edge of her writing, she is underlining a problem of great significance.

Critical history has rendered us aware that the ritual gestures we treasure owe their origin to human creativity in dialogue with divine revelation. Culturally they are human, temporal products. Consequently they are open to change, manipulation and reconstruction. Unquestionably the reconstruction of the Roman liturgy in the past 25 years has been one of the most daring—and most positive—expressions of cultural vibrancy in the church's history. But sometimes poets say better what is at issue than theologians or historians. Something has been lost in the shuffle. Poet Catherine De Vinck suggests what this might be in her poetic rendering of the eucharistic prayer:

God
    you are
        everywhere   anywhere   nowhere
        to be seen.

Out of chambers and streets
    of many lives, of many years
we come
    preciously holding what we saved:
a little wheel of bread
image of the endless circling of our hungers;
a splash of wine
in a cup where the sun of all our thirsts
trembles and shines. . . .

    Take and eat: this is my body.

He makes the time
        improvises the place:
he speaks himself into earth   water
                      air   fire. . . .

> He marks the time
>> improvises the place
>> speaks himself alive
>> in a flake of bread.[4]

Somehow we must learn again how to evoke the cosmic picture that is the nerve center of our worship. God is acting in the miracle of many families sharing life together. The unique, eternal, self-giving God who upholds the awesome reality of our fragile, magnificent universe gives "God-life" to those who are willing to come together in God's name to acknowledge and praise our solidarity with God in the one chosen and sent, Jesus the Christ.

A huge agenda of ritual enculturation remains. We must link scriptural word with experienced mystery and link random community with redemptive destiny. Until we celebrate the cosmic implications of our life and worship and appreciate the full scope of the texts of the Bible and the prayers of the liturgy, something integral is lacking in our sacramental life and in our church catechesis.

The agenda of ritual enculturation is most pressing, in fact, for the clergy. Many who were formed in an older Roman liturgy have been disoriented by the renewal; many others formed by the contemporary seminary have never dealt with aesthetic and anthropological dimensions of worship in any depth. But whether for clergy or others, the best context in which to hope for a repossession of our symbolic heritage is, in fact, the restored catechumenate.

The *what* of ritual life, in terms of our communal understanding of the saving mystery of Christian worship, is too often anemic and thin. As we move to the other aspects of ritual and sacramental catechesis, we cannot forget that this dimension is in need of ongoing attention and reconstruction.

Readiness for Ritual:
Cognitive Reconstruction of Worship

In addressing children's readiness for catechesis in an ecology of worship, we must keep many dimensions in mind at once.

Children become spontaneously curious about the world that surrounds them at the same time that they become less dependent on care givers who once provided all-embracing security linked to close physical presence. As children become less circumscribed by parental care, they enter wider circles of institutional involvements, which connect them with new persons and new events. For most of childhood, all book learning and formal classroom learning will be conditioned by the two-way street of relational transformation: growing detachment from parental security relations and growing attachment to figures in a widening circle of relations in school, play groups and early work experiences. Needless to say, parents remain fundamental figures in mediating all these changes throughout the entire period of childhood.

Affiliative Inclusion. A good way to open a discussion about the importance of feelings of connectedness in the lives of children might be to review some of the research of psychologist Jean Piaget, who for five decades explored the growth of logic in the lives of children. Piaget's use of terminology is unique to himself. He had a very particular perspective on consciousness, holding that human knowing begins at birth. So the seemingly random movements of an infant's hands and body are, for Piaget, initiation into the beginnings of human learning. The child must learn how to gain control over the musculature of the body and, doing so, prepare the way for later mobility and language usage. We may find it amusing to watch a small baby strain to yawn or to make facial expressions. We focus more spontaneously on the infant's amazing similarity to adult gestures and less on the evident effort that is reflected in the child's actions. But these actions are effortful, in no small part because the child is not only expressing physical behavior, but is also taking possession of a mastery of the body that must be learned and perfected.[5]

Once the first level of human knowing/learning, which Piaget called sensorimotor cognition, has been established, children are prepared to learn language. Early language is built on imitation and repetition, as we have all experienced in observing children's growth. Early language use often seems precocious to adults, because children are so oriented at this stage to imitation. What small children imitate, of course, is the language they hear adults use around them (including sophisticated language from TV and radio). Language is used here to share a world of belonging with attractive, more sophisticated adults. Language functions in human conversation as reciprocal input in an ongoing project of cooperation and co-construction of a shared world. Children seek inclusion within this attractive and dynamic project of conversation before they are fully skilled in logic and language, even if they do not fully comprehend what is at issue in a given moment of exchange. And, of course, we encourage children to do this, rightly imagining that we are helping them improve their linguistic and logical skills by doing so as desirous as they are of keeping them involved in the network of shared meanings.

Children understandably seek identification with adults who are more skilled than themselves. Their parents and other close adult figures are attractive for many reasons. They are life givers, providing security—and, in the case of parents, so vitally connected to children's experiences of safety as to seem irreplaceable. These same adults are bigger, more skilled and thereby symbols of what children imagine themselves becoming in due time. They are also centers of control, exercising the power of authority in the home and other forms of authority in other contexts. Adults represent larger meanings of life that may be subtle, but they are powerful shapes of consciousness and goals for growing children.

Ethnicity, class and vocational ideals are perceived by children in indirect ways. It appears that all children go through periods in which their family and parental heritage are felt to be superlative and worthy of defending against any— even imagined—slight from peers. Smaller children seem to need to claim, "My Daddy is better than yours; my Mommy is prettier—a better cook—smarter." Older children express similar dynamics in their chauvinistic expression of heritage through dress, language or affectations of other sorts. Of course, as children approach teen years, their tribe becomes the youth cohort and affiliative energies move more principally in the direction of identification with the peer group.

But enough has been suggested to indicate how vitally important the dynamic of affiliative inclusion is here. Imitation is central in the children's lives. Gradually children become more conscious and more in control of the dynamics of inclusion through imitation. But *belonging* is a central issue in both psychosocial development and in religious catechesis. Finding ways of expressing this native hunger for affiliation among our young so as to include them within the life and activities of the church community is a central challenge for our catechesis.[6]

Imaginative Reconstruction of Experience. The fact that children inhabit a significant period of life in which their conversation is more oriented toward social inclusion than toward logical understanding helps us to recognize another important factor in childhood maturation. The transformation of meanings children assign to experience is dependent not only on teaching or instruction but also on the constant shifting of perspective that comes with greater experience and increased exposure to a variety of attitudes and points of view.

We seldom stop to recognize that our human use of language is highly controlling. By naming, of course, we make it possible to refer to and even "manipulate" objects without having recourse to their physical presence. But as our desire to communicate engages more complex phenomena, our use of language likewise becomes more complicated. Thus in naming, we narrow our grasp on the untamed reality of an object at the same time that we extend our capacity to manipulate the same object through language. Things are always more than we can say about them.

Another useful idea of Piaget's is his conception of *centering* and *decentering*. Prelogical thought is "centered" in the sense that the focus of children is centered on their own experience.[7] A typical Piaget test for centered thinking is the following. A 4-year-old boy is asked: "Do you have a brother?"

The child answers: "Yes." "What is his name?" "Tommy." "Okay, well tell me then: Does Tommy have a brother?" To which the four-year-old answers: "No." From the centered viewpoint of this child, "Tommy" can be called a brother, but this child has never been put in the situation before of having to think of himself potentially as a brother to someone else.

Centered thinking is owed to limited experience and a small capacity to synthesize what has been experienced. Part of cognitive growth between the ages of 5 and 8 is the increased ability to hold fragments of experience together. Hand-eye coordination is part of this cognitive growth, but another part is a deeper penetration into the meaning of things and a deeper capacity to care, generated in part by increased curiosity about what makes things work.

"Decentering" is constantly in process. We decenter when we take a broader perspective, see things from others' points of view and grow in our ability to put that information together with our own view of things and come up with a transformed whole. Decentering, then, depends on growth in experience and increasing ability to integrate or synthesize fragments of experience. As children spontaneously develop in this ability, they re-process the meaning of their early learning and early feelings.

Another factor in imaginative reconstruction is the power of images to move affections. Psychologists who study memory claim that every image has a motor dynamic.[8] We are moved—perhaps only subliminally—by the images that impinge on our vision. While children experience prelogical cognition, powerful images are able to exert lasting influence on the contours of numinosity in their religious life. Without having the capacity to be self-reflective about such matters, small children nonetheless can be powerfully moved by sacred space, ritual actions, religious icons, statues and vessels.

Magical thinking, of course, is most at home in a prelogical world, so it is not surprising to discover that prelogical children have a strong inclination toward something akin to superstition. Yet we must be tolerant of the multiple dimensions that operate in such a world of confused numinosity. While we cannot be content to encourage children to perdure in a magical world that contains powerful overtones of manipulation of sources of power, we still should try to identify the ground of numinosity—the sense of the holy—that underlies their piety.

Early images of religion—God, heaven, holiness—landscape the religious imagination of the child and become reference points for validity and attraction when new phenomena come into their experience. Because powerful images can exercise the role of criteria for morality and religious authenticity, we must be concerned to engage the world of images as effectively as we engage the world of words and actions.

In view of these reflections, I claim that children take away from ritual more than they are able to say. It is probably true of all of us to varying degrees, but it is especially true of children that their openness to religious experience is greater than even their awareness or focused attention would suggest. Children invest symbolically in rituals as instruments of transcendence. At a certain age (midchildhood), numinosity seems to have as much to do with personality as anything: Sister is very holy; Father is very reverent; Mass was very special because of the bishop's being there. Children invest more deeply when they are invited to become personally involved in special ways, although children have strong hokum detectors—so their involvement has to be genuine.

Today's children may need *summary* experiences of ritual along with clear interpretations. Like all of us, children need to have their attention pointedly fixed upon foundational symbols such as light, water, gestures, sacred space and the meaning of sacred song. But what is deepest comes naturally. All the while that cognitive growth goes on, symbolic reconstruction of a child's experience goes on as well. We need to ask how to take advantage of this powerful energizer in the lives of our Christian children.

Textual and Creedal Learning. These observations about children's development have clear implications for children's classroom and textual learning. At earlier stages of development, the imparting of information is secondary to the dynamics of inclusion within an affiliating group and to the programming of symbolic elements in the children's imaginations. Somewhere around age 7 or 8 children penetrate more logically and get to the adult meanings of words and gestures. That is when we begin to turn the schoolroom into a laboratory for social programming and introduce children to the basics of reading, writing and mathematics.

Psychologists distinguish between "recalling" memory and "appropriating" (integrating into one's life) memory. With the first, children are able to give back the verbal or mathematical formulas that they have learned, but one cannot count on their penetrating the content of these formulas. With appropriating memory, on the other hand, children develop insight into the meaning and implications of the content to which they have been exposed. For a long period of childhood education, children waver on a frontier between these two forms of memory and understanding. Personal inclination to particular areas of study or application may govern the degree of investment that children make, influencing the degree to which they go beyond recall toward appropriation.

Clearly, then, children's relation to any text will have more than one dimension. Words can serve purposes beyond mere information, although the information is of vital importance. But words can become a potent source for later reflection and later appropriation, even if at a given moment in the process of education those words remain relatively impenetrable. This should not surprise us, for our tradition knows a variety of examples that express the multiple dimensions of sacred texts.

The Latin word for creed, interestingly, was *symbolum*, suggesting that the words of the creeds are about far more than imparting information.[9] Like so many verbal formulas from religious traditions, creeds are more a sort of "textual icon" than a summary of information, though (again) I do not wish to deny the importance of the informational dynamic in the creedal process. But even within the canon of Holy Scripture, sacred texts are referred to as Holy Wisdom. Wisdom has multiple meanings, but I would claim in this context that its principal meaning is a teaching from a divine perspective or, put another way, a statement about reality that derives from the merciful revelation of God. Thus, in a way like the ten commandments, Holy Wisdom says as much about the fact that God can and does speak to a chosen people as it does about precise details of theology or policy.

Holy Wisdom as textual icon (the Sacred Scriptures as revelatory of God's love) has been celebrated in our time by the liturgical renewal in the practice of enthronement of the Bible. The Gospel Book is a text whose words make possible an opening of human hearts to the heart of God. In consequence, no one utterance or proclamation of these texts will be able to engage the full power of these holy words, for more is at issue than informing believers about the message in the divine utterance. Proclamation is an invitation whose power often surprises us because it is heard in the subtle depths of rumination (human pondering) and reflective concern.

Therefore it is fairly clear that two distinct things occur together, linked to one another but not in a particular order. First is the proclamation or presentation of the textual icon. It can be heard as just another incidental claim on one's attention; it may be received as a message from God but remain inert and incomprehensible. It can also explode into a call to sensitive cooperation with the action of God in the world and a touching awareness of the amazing immediacy of God's merciful love. When that happens—it *can't* happen without proclamation—a new order of reality comes to be.

Children in the simplicity of their incomplete appropriation of gospel meaning can nonetheless arrive at this demanding awareness of the immediacy of God's call and God's merciful love. In any case, children (like the rest of us) only gradually penetrate and appropriate the textual icon—its words, its meanings and its implications. But we need to aim at communicating the integrity of the complex reality of divine address from the beginning. The question for us in the present context is how this can be done. How can we maintain at all times both logical (reasonable, rational) and symbolic (prelogical, at the level of image) dimensions vibrantly alive?

Why Children Want to Worship, to Learn, to Grow

Motivation for moral and religious development is a question clouded in ambiguity in the literature of moral development. Piaget and Kohlberg both used the formula, "cognitive disequilibrium." This term describes the strain or stress that results when existing structures of thought and behavior no longer serve to provide children access to experiences and actions in which they want to take part. Then, better structures are needed. Both Piaget and Kohlberg appear to have held for a strong maturational agenda: They understood this cognitive disequilibrium as a continuing, necessary by-product of growth, though they also noted well that not all cognitive disequilibrium resulted in growth. Both believed that there are typical structures of cognition, affection and behavior that pertain to human life and that, given need and proper stimulation, people will move forward to more satisfactory stages.[10] Their theory presupposed an innate hunger for meaning ("epistemological libido") growing ever more complex, ever more curious and ever more subtle in its capacity to differentiate the qualities of experience.

While I agree with the general lines of such a theory of cognitive disequilibrium, I do not find it sufficient. It is too extrinsic and too simplistic an account; it does not say enough about where this hunger for meaning comes from or why and how it must be transformed. For the present, I would like to suggest a view of development that describes how community involvement through ritual gradually moves children toward the moment when they own or take responsibility for their ritual tradition.

Like every other aspect of human socialization, religious ritual life is at first quasi-coercive (when you're a child, you do things because your parents require it). One is introduced into the ritual process by caretakers. We know that some Christian communities have opposed infant baptism for the reason that, in their view, ritual participation ought to be fully conscious and fully appropriated. Yet, from the fourth century, many Christians were initiated as infants, and—one suspects—

many adult converts knew as little as infants about why they were adopting the religion of their warlord or prince.

However ritual initiation is begun, eventually all participants will distance themselves to some degree from a coercive introduction to ritual life. Some spontaneous movements of the human spirit typically occur in childhood. Early grade-school children often intuit a sense of God, a felt acknowledgment of their dependency on their Creator for the origin of their lives. This may be promoted by some experience of vulnerability or may be a natural reflection on the language and rites of the religious community in which they grow up. Later, children develop genuine, personally initiated questions about the origin and destiny of their lives.

In the midst of this dialectic between externally initiated influences and spontaneously developing religious curiosity, children also develop a life of religious emotions that responds to their perceived understandings of God. Children know emotions of gratitude, love and desire for union with God that are genuine in the sense that they are not just parroting others' words and descriptions but are experiencing true feelings that move them deeply and lastingly.

There is, of course, a parallel here between these religious emotions and children's filial attachment to parents. As we saw previously, children have to deal with issues involving security, personality fusion and psychological control. Just as parents symbolize an archaic experience of absolute dependency and absolute security for the child, so does God. Just as parental dependency as an issue eventually leads to adolescent withdrawal and resistance, so does "God imagery" of absolute theological dependency lead to distancing from the faith in many cases. The sheer fact of "being controlled" absolutely—by God or parents or anyone else—becomes intolerable for some adolescents.

This development typically continues with youth "seeing through" (calling into question) their childhood religious motivation. Most atheists become atheists because they are scandalized by the inadequacy of their own images of God. What they fail to see is that they are accomplices to the crime of defining the godhead in such insufficient terms. They likewise fail to appreciate that there are theological and poetic alternatives to naming God and reaching out to a hidden God.

This critical process of reworking images of God can begin as early as late childhood. The sacral agenda of the churches comes into conflict with the educational agenda of the schools. Functional social education is oriented toward establishing matter-of-fact empirical connections between experienced phenomena and possible physical causes. One of the classic issues for centuries, repeated almost inevitably in the educational life of almost every religious child, is the clash between different genres of expression.

So much ritual and theological talk is couched in poetic and metaphorical language. When one struggles to understand basic concepts of physics, it can be fairly easy to ridicule religious romanticism in the name of hardheaded science. Of course, this clash has to occur and, properly handled, is not only beneficial but imperative for a realistic religious vision. But we know from experience that this conflict is not always properly handled and that, in consequence, a number of students—often the brightest ones—are lost to religion because there is no one there to help them through their struggle to disenchant a fundamentalist religious perspective.

Children likewise observe mixed levels of performance and commitment in the adults around them. To be asked to behave religiously when the controlling figures themselves are inconsistent in their religious attitudes is galling to youth. This is all very familiar ground, but it takes its toll all the same.

Somehow, therefore, we must find a way to help older children work through their God issues. We must give them a forum to sort through the inconsistencies we refer to here. Religious discourse being what it is, children may not themselves be aware that there is a latent disaffection beneath the surface of their thoughts and feelings. And as before—but even more importantly in the early teen years—youth greatly depend on their peer group for reference and support.

There are many ways that we can meet this transition to critical consciousness in youth. One way, which is often decisive in bringing teens into deeper relation with the worshiping community, is to provide them with roles within the ritual and the community's actions. There are moments in which it would be appropriate to offer them opportunities to proclaim the word in the eucharistic assembly, to serve at rites or to prepare community gatherings. We do no one a favor, however, if we do this in a spirit of tokenism and include them without demanding quality performance from them. Someone must take responsibility to assure that such moments of high profile participation by the young are also moments of recognized competence as well.

To summarize this point, motivation for religious participation will shift through the childhood years. It begins with the desire to be a valued part of the whole. To that is added gradually deeper spontaneous intellectual motivation. But the desire to know for the sake of quenching curiosity will never altogether be divorced from the relational links. Our celebration of the way we think the world is put together is also a celebration of the basic network of human partners whose attitudes and interests are closest to our own. Sometimes this will lead to painful tension, as when youth finds it impossible to reconcile parental views with the dominant views of peers or of authorities outside the family circle.

In trying to get a grasp on this immensely complex interactive framework, we should remember that we have to work not only with articulate words—textual icons, as I called them earlier—but also with the imaginative landscapes that underlie and energize attested ideas. This is very hard. A question, difficult to grasp and probably even more difficult to realize, might be whether or not our working through practical experiences of ritualization with paraliturgical use of material symbols might enlarge young people's appreciation for both the power and the subtlety of ritual life. It would take a theologian who is also a magician to achieve such a difficult enterprise. Or, who knows? Perhaps it would only take convincing and consistent catechesis within a ritual ecology. Perhaps one of the questions for a consideration of children's catechesis within the context of the catechumenate is how we can verify that we always maintain a physical/symbolic component in every stage of the catechesis of textual icons.

Conclusion

I have tried to open up a wide sample of perspectives on religious development. In doing so, I freely referred to common-sense views in the same breath that I raised research findings. Methodologically this is a problem. On the other hand, I hope that my observations have served to reshape the familiar rather than introduce a lot of new ideas. In any case, allow me to close with a list of tasks for catechesis of children in a ritual ecology—such as the catechumenal parish can become.

Welcome. We welcome children into a world of Christian celebration. We communicate to them: "Here, this is our world with God in Christ." Their sense of the presence of God in the church is mediated by our manifest signs of belief. As the French school of catechetics said in the 1940s: "The faith of the catechist is the motive of credibility for the catechumens."

Awaken. We awaken the latent sense of God in their lives. We attest: "Children, we are God's people and this is how we are brought together by God's word and action." We say what we understand to be taking place in the mysteries that we celebrate.

Include. We include children as integral partners in the fully serious pursuit of responding to God in our family, neighborhood, parish and community. We say: "These are the mysteries given us by God to make us one family. Here is how we serve our God; come help us do that."

Instruct. We instruct our children, to help them decipher the already potent world of experience that they carry within themselves. We assist them in knowing the multiple layers of religious experience. We say: "Our God is a hidden God. God has spoken through revealed words and in the living Jesus who became the Christ. God speaks in your heart in prayer and yearning. God speaks through the church to integrate all the elements of human living into the Christian mystery—to assure the balance of all things in one universal whole."

Forgive, Liberate, Unite and Empower. We also forgive, liberate, unite and empower the children and youth, and we ask them to follow suit: "God's word tells us that the Holy Spirit will live within us, that our actions can reveal the presence of God. Together we are church, making God visible within our own time and space. In such a world shared with God, see yourselves transformed: See your world transfigured. Everything that does not belong to this new world of union with God will wither away and die. But with forgiveness, everything old and unworthy can be set aside and new life begun in the promise of communion with God. When we awaken to this mystery, we become the one body in Christ, and this new unity also gives us access to all the power that God showed us in the revelation of Christ."

The Function of Catechesis. The tasks for catechesis described here are functions. These functions are not exercised by reciting these words—or words like them. Yet those of us who have worked with children know that they need to be welcomed, awakened, included, instructed and empowered. Perhaps my previous remarks will suggest how all these functions must employ many levels of expression from verbal and logical to symbolic and imaginative. The joy of catechizing in a ritual ecology is the recognition that, because of the diversity and multiplicity of religious communication, all the members of the catechumenal community can profit—each in their own way—from one common celebration of word and sacrament. When that conviction is achieved, much of what is needed to welcome children into the conversion contract is already at hand.

NOTES

1. Annie Dillard, *Teaching a Stone to Talk* (New York: Harper and Row, 1982), 19–20.

2. See "Axis Mundi," in *The Encyclopedia of Religion,* vol. 2, Mircea Eliade, editor in chief (New York: Macmillan Co., 1987), 20–21; see Kees W. Bolle, "Speaking of a Place," in *Myths and Symbols,* ed. J. M. Kitigawa and C. H. Long (Chicago: The University of Chicago Press, 1969), 127–40.

3. Dillard, *Teaching a Stone to Talk,* 31–33.

4. Catherine De Vinck, "A Liturgy," *Cross Currents* 23 (Fall 1973): 268–69.

5. Jean Piaget, *Six Psychological Studies,* trans. Anita Tenzer (New York: Vintage Books, 1968).

6. See John H. Westerhoff and Gwen K. Neville, *Generation to Generation* (New York: Pilgrim Press, 1979), 11–106.

7. See *The Essential Piaget,* ed. H. E. Gruber and J. J. Voneche (New York: Basic Books, 1977), 439–44.

8. See Paul Philibert, "The Promise and Perils of Memorization," *The Living Light* 17 (Winter 1980): 299–310.

9. Joseph Ratzinger, *Introduction to Christianity,* trans. J. R. Foster (New York: Herder and Herder, 1970), 50–64.

10. See *The Essential Piaget,* 832–37.

CHAPTER
13

" *A child is led in the catechumenal journey
to discover a relationship with God through
the person of Jesus. Authentic conversion in our
tradition puts the person of Jesus Christ
at the center.* **"**

Discerning
Conversion
in Children

ROBERT D. DUGGAN

P astoral experience with the implementation of the
Rite of Christian Initiation of Adults (RCIA) shows
the centrality of conversion within the whole order.
Communities that take seriously the challenge of
the RCIA are drawn swiftly and inexorably to face the
challenge of conversion not only for the candidates and catechumens but for themselves as well. One of the earliest questions in
such communities is inevitably that of how best to discern—as
well as minister to a person with—an authentic experience of
Christian conversion.

One of the fundamental points when raising the question of
conversion in the context of the initiation of children is the
normative status of the adult rite. That the initiation of children of catechetical age is treated within the context of an adult
initiation ritual is not without significance. It is conversion
sketched in its fullest expression through the rites and periods
of the adult experience that gives shape and definition to a
corresponding experience for children. Pastoral and theological
commentators often have observed that the RCIA enjoys a
normative status for the church's initiatory policy. This holds
true in many regards not only for the implications of its ritual

praxis, its pastoral care, its ministerial structures, its ecclesial vision, but also for its understanding of conversion.

This author has written elsewhere about the adult experience of conversion, and that material will not be repeated here. See the entries in "For Further Reading" at the end of this collection. In addition, the remarks here are best understood in the context of the related chapter by Paul Philibert in this collection. His insights are rich and provocative in their implications for discerning conversion in children, and this chapter can only allude to some of those implications.

Discernment

Before discussing discernment of conversion in children, some preliminary remarks are in order concerning discernment generally. The context in which discernment takes place is always one of prayer. Openness to the Spirit and a sense of being in the presence of God are essential qualities for those who engage in a process of discernment. Any formal session at which a catechumenal team undertakes to discern the experience of conversion in a candidate begins with quiet for prayer, explicit invocation of the Spirit and a conscious effort to still the competing voices that distract from a focus on God's presence.

A discernment session, then, is more like a faith assembly than a business meeting. It is more concerned with listening than with problem solving. It is more a right-brain experience than a left-brain one. The operative assumption is not that there is a puzzle to be solved but that God is speaking, leading, revealing divine truth, and our task is simply to listen attentively and respond faithfully.

We speak here of a "formal" session of discernment, but it must be remembered that discernment is an ongoing reality in every catechumenal process. There will, of course, be special moments that a team sets aside for this task, such as before the major transitional rites. But throughout the candidate's journey, various members of the team, whether their role is sponsor, catechist or whatever, feel a responsibility for viewing a candidate from God's perspective, for uncovering God's action in the child's life. In setting the yearly schedule for the team, plans should be made for those formal moments of discernment but also for times when a team is assisted with its continuing responsibility for ongoing discernment in less formal ways.

Discernment is a communal responsibility, not just the job of one or two team members. In fact, the broader the base of involvement in this process, the better. Structures adequate—but not too elaborate—to the challenge of involving a number of individuals in the process are needed. The text addresses the possibility of involving other members of the catechumenal community in the discernment process (RCIA, 122). This can be more difficult to do with children than with adults, but the difficulty should not discourage efforts in that direction. At the very least, the candidates themselves should feel involved in the community's effort to recognize how God has worked in their lives. The attempt to do such listening can itself deepen conversion in a child's life.

Discernment is both purifying and enlightening. Like the scrutinies, discernment relies on God's power for its success. It is an act of trust that God reveals what must be known and seen. And often the very experience of bringing to light what still remains to be healed can begin a process of purification. Also like scrutinies, discernment is fearless before God's truth, even when that truth is painful to confront. The gospel ever retains its countercultural elements, and those who pray for what is needed for conversion to be complete must remain open to the answer that comes forth. At the same time, especially with children, those who discern are mindful of the gradual, progressive, ongoing nature of conversion. Discernment always challenges individuals to further growth, but God's time is not human time, and neither the rhythm nor the pace of the forward movement can be predetermined. Developmentalists may be able to predict the sequence of human growth stages on a variety of levels, but the mystery of conversion, while it operates within the context of those developmental stages, always eludes mere identification with them.

If conversion in children is intertwined with, but not the same as, growth and development, then we must seek to understand its specificity. Discernment is based on the ability to recognize the shape of authentic conversion. Therefore, the remainder of our remarks are concerned with understanding conversion and how to recognize its contours in children moving through the catechumenal journey.

Conversion

Conversion is a relative notion. It is accommodated to the appropriate developmental level of the child at any given age. Our discernment and our evaluation of conversion misses the mark if we forget this.

Another helpful reminder, before we look more closely at some specific elements in the experience of conversion, is that certain pastoral consequences flow from any particular understanding of conversion. What follows has definite implications for pastoral ministry designed to support conversion of a particular sort. Although our task here is not to describe these implications, the reader is urged to read between the lines and recognize the direction that pastoral ministry might take in light of this understanding of conversion.

Conversion Is Entrance into a Covenant. When the RCIA uses the language of covenant to describe conversion, it is borrowing scriptural "code" language to indicate that conversion is always a relational dynamic. Conversion is interpersonal. It is about the establishment of a network of saving relationships. The RCIA calls the child into a series of such relationships. The cornerstone of the experience of conversion is the issue of whether or not the child has entered a vital relationship with God. Has the child discovered God as one who has initiated a love relationship with her or him on a very personal level? The RCIA insists that this be the case, that in the person of Jesus, we discover the face of a God who invites us into a deep personal relationship. That relationship, of course, is not with God alone, but with God *incarnate* in the body of Christ, the church.

Another element of the biblical notion of covenant applies here: From the human side any response to God's call must be a free one. The notion of conversion that the RCIA embodies underlines this freedom of the individual to respond to the divine initiative. In discerning the nature of conversion in a child, therefore, we seek and encourage signs of freedom. Paul Philibert's remarks about the images that "landscape the religious imagination of the child" remind us that a child's images of God must be noncoercive. The experience of conversion, in the religious imagination of the child, involves an offer that is not threatening, one that is truly an invitation. Similarly, the task of the catechumenal team is to discern whether or not the emotional tonality with which the child responds is characterized by whatever level of freedom is appropriate for the child's age and stage of development.

Conversion Is Radically Christocentric. As we said previously, a child is led in the catechumenal journey to discover a relationship with God through the person of Jesus. Authentic conversion in our tradition puts the person of Jesus Christ at the center. If there is anything or anyone else at the heart of the experience, then the conversion is to some extent faulty, and further pastoral care must be exercised to assist the child to place Jesus—and the story of Jesus—at the heart of his or her religious development. The journey of conversion for a child must be filled with stories of Jesus. Depending on the particular age of the child and her or his age-specific developmental interests, certain stories of Jesus will be more or less appropriate. Whether Jesus is presented as the great hero to which young adolescents gravitate so readily, as the revolutionary, as one who challenges the political, religious and social structures of the day, or whether the image offered is of Jesus the good shepherd, Jesus leading, guiding, supporting and protecting the flock—all must be determined on an individual basis. What is fundamental to discerning conversion in the child is whether or not the child has come to understand and appropriate a relationship with Jesus as the heart and center of the Christian experience.

Conversion Is Essentially Ecclesial. The RCIA affirms that initiation involves insertion into a community of faith. The communal nature of the initiation process is so obvious and well known that it requires little comment here. However, it is perhaps helpful to connect this insight with remarks made by Paul Philibert regarding affiliative inclusion and its centrality for the developing religious experience of the child. Philibert also reminds us of the complexity involved in the adolescent's task of negotiating the necessary disengagement from parental and other authority structures while, at the same time, developing an expanding network of peer relationships in the broader world. Church, closely identified as it is with authority structures and parental value systems, can easily be a problematic issue for the young adolescent. All the more reason, then, to give a young person at that stage ample opportunity for distancing while still insisting that issues of personal faith and meaning be worked out and resolved within the context of the church. This issue of necessary disengagement, while still offering opportunities for affiliative inclusion, is critical for catechesis with the emerging adolescent. For this reason we can understand how valuable a peer group and peer ministry are to the ongoing conversion of young people. The larger community or the other levels of community that are involved in the young person's full experience of church also must in some meaningful way remain present. Those who must discern the adequacy of the child's experience of conversion are well advised to evaluate just what dynamics are operative in the child's relationship with the church on all of these levels of community and of personal conduct.

Conversion Is Fundamentally Sacramental. The RCIA views conversion as a radically sacramental experience. This means both that the experience is not a purely interior one—that it must be externalized, it must be "sacramentalized"—and that the process of conversion is carried forward in and by rituals, our sacramental rites. Religious ritual, then, is integral to the experience and is required for a full and authentic expression of conversion, no less for the child than for the adult. This insight, it seems, is often at odds with the prevailing notion of conversion in our society. The "altar call" of certain evangelical traditions, the "baptism in the Spirit" of certain charismatic traditions, the "making Christ the center of my life" of certain fundamentalist traditions and the "born-again" phenomenon in several traditions—many of these view conversion as basically a private, interior event, something that occurs between "Jesus and me" at the depths of my being. The liturgical and evangelical-liturgical traditions such as Roman Catholicism and others view authentic conversion as ongoing, visibly expressed and carried forward through sacramental celebrations such as those that the RCIA offers.

In this light, it is easy to underline the importance of Paul Philibert's insights into the importance of ritual enculturation of children. Our task, in his view, is to strive to "engage the world of images as effectively as we engage the world of words and actions." In this writer's opinion, Philibert's claim that children "take away from ritual more than they are able to say" is correct. In fact, it is sustenance for a lifetime that they carry away from our sacramental celebrations. A child's conversion experience must constantly be fed with ritual and nourished with our primary symbols of death-resurrection, birth-rebirth, creation-recreation, darkness-light. Children must be immersed in and caught up in ritual expressions where the heart of the meaning is clearly encountering a loving God and opening up to the love that God offers. Philibert contends that the proclamation of the "textual icon" can mediate for the child the "demanding awareness" of the immediacy of God's call. Clearly, the sacramental moment of proclamation is the privileged locus for this encounter and heightens the urgency for a more developed experience of children's celebrations of the word on Sunday and feasts as well as at other points in the catechumenal journey.

In discerning the adequacy of a child's conversion experience in this regard, then, we look at both the breadth and depth of the ritual experience offered to the child and for evidence that an assimilation commensurate with the age and understanding of the child has occurred.

Conversion Is a Spiritual Journey. Once again the RCIA uses the language of scripture to convey an important spiritual insight, namely that conversion occurs gradually. This counters the popular notion in our society that conversion is an *event* rather than a *process*. Some Christian traditions emphasize their ability to name the specific moment when members "received the Lord." This view could distort both our understanding of conversion and the way we give support through pastoral ministry. The RCIA views conversion as a phenomenon with rhythms and stages; and, while it may be punctuated by moments of greater or lesser intensity, it is understood as ongoing. A further consequence of this notion of conversion as a spiritual journey is that the particular stage at which a child finds herself or himself requires that pastoral efforts and all else be accommodated to the appropriate level. Pastoral ministers can be impatient with children no less than with themselves and can easily yield to the temptation to rush a process that requires slow, gradual growth. The result and danger, of course, is that we invoke mere conformity rather than genuine conversion from the children. Children are eager to please— sometimes to a fault—and quick to imitate what is perceived to be desired by the adult community. For this reason it is a constant struggle to invite rather than subtly coerce, to support and encourage, but to stop short of imposing and insisting.

Here the insights of the developmentalists are crucial. We must know what a child is capable of at each stage and seek no more than that. We wait patiently for the seed to mature, confident that in God's time and with God's grace authentic conversion will lead to mature faith. But we refuse to try to rush that process.

We also recognize the importance of regressive moments. As indicated previously, adolescents in particular often need space in which to create distance, precisely as part of their process of development. The developmentalists provide us here with a clearer understanding of what we already knew as theologians: Failure, rebellion and sin are the raw material out of which we discover a life of grace based on experiences of reconciliation and forgiveness.

Conversion Is a Total Transformation in a Person. The human sciences once again come to our aid with their reminder that the human being is a unity embracing cognitive, affective and behavioral dimensions. Growth and development occur on all of these levels, often in parallel fashion, often intertwined intimately. This reminder focuses our attention on the multiple dimensions of change and the many levels on which conversion occurs in the life of a child. Sensitive ministry to the conversion experience of the child requires that our discernment, as well as our pastoral care, be nuanced and multifaceted. For too long religious education has been lopsidedly preoccupied with the cognitive. What is needed is a shift of paradigm in which the pastoral care of children will replace a narrow "religious education mind-set" with a far broader concern for "initiation." As Catherine Dooley, Berard Marthaler and John Westerhoff state in their chapters in this collection, conversion is more than religious literacy. The academic mold that still dominates our approach to religious education of children is invariably preoccupied with religious literacy. Pastoral care of children that has as its focus their initiation into a faith community, on the other hand, tends to free up ministers to care more broadly for the affective and behavioral dimensions.

What is necessary is balance, both in our ministry to the child's multileveled experience as well as to the child's progressive transformation on all of those levels. In the child, as in the adult, we look for signs of a deepening of the affective bonding with God and with God's people. We play "matchmaker" between the child and our God of love revealed in the sacred stories of covenant. We introduce the child to a series of relationships in the church, relationships that we want to grow and flourish in a climate of love and caring. We also look for behavioral evidences that testify to values internalized. Aware of the developmental stages in which the child naturally seeks approval through conformity, we nonetheless recognize those spontaneous movements of goodness that flow from a generous heart.

Conclusion

In this chapter we offered some suggestions about discernment and how it ought to operate in the communal context of a catechumenate. We attempted to delineate some of the contours of the conversion experience as grounded in adult initiation but found in parallel fashion in the experience of children. We also suggested a few of the features that might stand out, as those who minister to the child on a journey of conversion attempt to discern and support that experience. In all of this, of course, we remain mindful that we tread on sacred ground and deal with mystery. Those who minister with children know well the miracle of human growth and how the uniqueness of each child is a source of constant surprise and wonder. The individuality of every child is all the more evident when we see how her or his journey of faith involves the constant discovery and revelation of God. If we are faithful servants of this God in our ministry to children, the harvest will be abundant.

CHAPTER
14

> *"Initiation should always be full initiation. Whenever it is time to initiate a person into the church, the initiation should be complete, celebrated fully, with the rites in their proper sequence. If infants are to be baptized, they should be fully initiated like everybody else."*

Children's Initiation for the Future: Where Are We Going?

RICHARD P. MOUDRY

But that doesn't make sense, Father!" "Maybe not, Mae," her pastor replied, "but that's the way we do it in our parish." What occasioned this exchange? Mae, a middle-aged grandmother, was eagerly looking forward to her three grandchildren "getting their sacraments." Two of her grandchildren—twin girls—were being raised by her devout Catholic daughter and were ready for their first communion. Her other grandchild—a young boy—was the same age but had never been baptized; Mae's son and his wife had only recently returned to Catholic practice and were now ready to present their own son for baptism. Mae's three grandchildren were not just cousins but playmates and friends, and Mae was looking forward to their receiving the sacraments together—a great family event.

Inconsistent Sacramental Models in the Same Parish

It was what Mae found out from her pastor that caused her dismay. Her unbaptized grandson was going to be fully initiated into the church at the Easter Vigil that year, receiving baptism, confirmation and first communion. But her two baptized granddaughters would not be part of that event. They were expected to make first confession soon and would receive first communion later in the spring. Her baptized granddaughters would not be confirmed at all. Confirmation would come later, in high school. Her pastor was going to confirm her unbaptized grandson but said that he was not permitted to confirm the baptized granddaughters of the same age.

Mae recognized that her grandchildren were going to receive the sacraments in very different ways. Thus her reaction, "But that doesn't make sense, Father!"

What Mae didn't know was that the way her baptized granddaughters were going to receive the sacraments—first confession before first communion and confirmation at a later age—is actually the exception in our church practice. In the Eastern church, persons ready for baptism always have been baptized, confirmed and given first communion at the same time. In the Roman Catholic church of the West today, those who have reached catechetical age are baptized, confirmed and given first communion at the same time. Baptized Catholic Christians who were never instructed and raised in their faith or who practiced in another Christian denomination for a time but now wish to practice as Catholics complete initiation in confirmation and first communion together. Baptized Protestant Christians who wish to be Catholics are received by being confirmed and given communion together. In all of these categories of initiation, the priest is the minister of confirmation as well as of baptism and first communion. More so than Mae could have imagined, the way her Catholic grandchildren were going to receive the sacraments does not make sense.

What was true in Mae's parish is true in most Catholic parishes. We have two different ways of celebrating the sacraments with our children. For unbaptized children of catechetical age, we initiate fully—baptism, confirmation and first communion in one liturgy with the pastor as presider. For our baptized children of the same age, our practice changes: We add confession and only then give first communion, and we postpone confirmation by the bishop for up to a decade. The result?

Differences in the number (If some children receive baptism, confirmation and eucharist on the same day, is it one sacrament or three?) of the sacraments, the order of the sacraments, the time for their celebration and the minister of confirmation.

Each of these two practices is founded on different assumptions, on different understandings of the meaning of the sacraments and of their function in the life of a child and of the church. This leads, of course, to two different catecheses of the rites. All this in the same parish. Sometimes even in the very same family!

What are the understandings that underpin the two different ways we celebrate the sacraments with our children? One practice is based on an understanding of these sacraments as "childhood sacraments." The other practice is based on an understanding of these sacraments as "Christian initiation of children."

The "Childhood-Sacraments" Model

"Childhood sacraments" is the understanding that children receive the sacraments to gain the grace needed for the various stages of their development during childhood. It is inherent in this understanding that the sacraments are separated from one another by several years. The range of ages at which confirmation has been celebrated in recent decades results from various strategies about where in the process of a child's faith development this sacrament best functions.

The reasons for the discrete celebration of these sacraments involve the need for a distinct if not independent meaning for each sacrament in order to explain its function in the life of the child. Thus, a newborn urgently needs to be baptized for the removal of sin and for membership in the church. When a child can tell right from wrong, first confession is needed for the forgiveness of sins before first communion and as training in what is hoped will be a lifetime Catholic habit of dealing with human weakness and sin by means of the sacrament of penance. At the age of reason, a child receives first communion as the beginning of a new kind of closeness to Jesus. Finally, at the end of childhood when the young Catholic is prepared to speak and act on her or his own behalf, as the culmination of sacramental life, confirmation celebrates the special coming of the Holy Spirit to empower her or him for adult living in the church. Celebrated in isolation, each sacrament needs a meaning of its own.

Only from the early twentieth century to this day in most Catholic parishes, have we been celebrating baptism, first confession, first communion and confirmation—in that order and over a period of about 15 years—as "childhood sacraments."

The "Christian-Initiation-of-Children" Model

The other practice—celebrating baptism, confirmation and first communion together—is based on an understanding of these sacraments as the "Christian initiation of children."

The reform of Christian initiation was one of the major liturgical accomplishments of the Second Vatican Council. Central to this reform was the identification of baptism, confirmation and first communion as initiatory sacraments, rites that are to be celebrated together and in that order, rites that together constitute full Christian initiation. This vision of Christian initiation is most fully embodied and best illustrated in the Rite of Christian Initiation of Adults (RCIA), where this unified initiatory practice is established for unbaptized adults and unbaptized children of catechetical age, as well as for baptized but uncatechized adults who have not completed their full initiation and for baptized persons who are being received as Catholics.

In this initiatory understanding, baptism, confirmation and first communion are a cluster of rites that together celebrate a single, multifaceted reality, the initial experience of the paschal mystery—a new birth, the beginning of a new life, coming to belong to the church, membership in the Sunday assembly. In this understanding, the sacraments must be celebrated together as one event, instead of being separated by years. It is the three symbols celebrated together—water bath with imposition of hands and anointing leading to table—that express the one paschal reality and constitute Christian initiation. And because they are sacraments of initiation, they are celebrated at the *start* of Christian life in the church, at whatever age that start happens.

Because initiatory sacraments are celebrated as a single event rather than separately, it is not necessary to identify independent meanings for the sacraments, nor does the RCIA require it. For example, confirmation, rather than being a conclusion or culmination or graduation, functions to confirm the water bath and lead to the table. The Holy Spirit is present in the life-giving water of baptism and at the eucharistic table fellowship, indeed in the whole initiatory process, rather than in some special way at confirmation celebrated separately. Christian mission is a consequence of baptism, and empowerment for apostolic living is a function of the eucharist.

The RCIA insists that first communion, rather than being an early childhood, intermediate sacrament, functions as the "culminating point" (RCIA, 217), the "climax" (RCIA, 243) of Christian initiation. The water bath and chrismation rites by their very nature seek completion in the final symbol of becoming a member of the body of Christ: joining the faithful at the table of the Lord. The goal of Christian initiation is the Sunday eucharistic assembly. That Sunday gathering is the springboard for mission.

Mixed Signals on Confirmation

In our practice based on the childhood-sacraments model, it is only in this century that the sacrament of confirmation has come to be located *after* first communion. That practice persists today, even though it is out of step with the initiatory theology and practice of a 1,900-year tradition and the renewed RCIA. The 1971 reformed Rite of Confirmation (RC) reaffirms the practice of delaying confirmation until about the age of seven (RC, 11), but it does not authorize postponing confirmation until after first communion.

A 1988 addition by the United States Catholic Conference to the RCIA envisions a situation where baptized Catholic children of catechetical age complete initiation in the same ceremony at which their unbaptized peers are fully initiated:

> Baptized children of the catechetical group may be completing their Christian initiation in the sacraments of confirmation and the eucharist at this same celebration [If the sacraments of initiation are celebrated at a time other than the Easter Vigil or Easter Sunday, the Mass of the day or one of the ritual Masses in the Roman Missal, "Christian Initiation: Baptism," is used (RCIA, 306).] When the bishop himself will not be the celebrant, he should grant the faculty to confirm such children to the priest who will be the celebrant (See RC, Introduction, 7). For their confirmation, previously baptized children of the catechetical group are to have their own sponsors. If possible, these should be the persons who were godparents for their baptism, but other qualified persons may be chosen (see RC, 5 and 6). (RCIA, 308)

Surely this is an effort to locate confirmation before first communion and thus reduce the inconsistency between our two sacramental practices. In the 1986 National Statutes for the Catechumenate (NSC), there is a recommendation that unbaptized children of catechetical age share in some of the sacramental preparation of their baptized peers—but with caution: Do not change the sequence of the sacraments determined in the ritual (NSC, 19), virtually a warning against the unbaptized children being "infected" by the common practice of delaying confirmation until after first communion.

In many dioceses of our country, teenage confirmation has been allowed under the provision in canon 891. This provision successfully preserves our practice of childhood sacraments, but its effect is to force parishes to continue the practice of confirmation after first communion, a practice that is clearly inconsistent with ritual and canonical norms. It will be interesting to see whether the National Conference of Catholic Bishops (NCCB) will continue to allow this "exceptional" practice of teenage confirmation, especially after their promulgation (NSC, 29), which interprets canon 842, §2 as defining "the interrelationship and sequence of confirmation and eucharist." For the moment, the NCCB both declares that confirmation comes before first communion and permits teenage confirmation. Without change, that could result in teenage first communion!

Anachronistic Practice

In the face of the glaring inconsistencies between the practice of childhood sacraments and the practice of initiatory sacraments, it is a tribute to the strength of our attachment to childhood sacraments that the practice has been so little questioned during the almost 20 years since the promulgation of the RCIA. "Childhood sacraments" remain our usual parish practice, an important purpose of parochial schools and a given in the design of grade-school-religion curricula. How long will our current practice of childhood sacraments be able to withstand the influence of the initiatory understanding of baptism, confirmation and first communion that comes from our long tradition, and includes the RCIA?

Moving Toward Consistency

Since the promulgation of the RCIA, we have come to face an even more radical anomaly in sacramental practice. Except for infants, no longer can we think of baptizing someone without immediately going on to confirmation and first communion: complete initiation. But with infants, we continue to celebrate baptism alone, as a birth sacrament, according to the rationale of childhood sacraments: incomplete initiation. The RCIA sharpens this inconsistency but does not resolve it.

The question is not, "Should we continue to baptize infants, or should we wait to baptize children when they are more mature?" Rather, the question is, "When we baptize infants, why do we leave their initiation incomplete, to be celebrated piecemeal over the next decade and more?" What is the meaning of initiation when it takes 16 years to complete? Does initiation have one meaning for infants (helping parents raise their children as Catholics) but a different meaning for all others (the start of Christian life)? As a rite of initiation, what does baptism practiced alone, without the other two initiatory sacraments, mean? What is there about being initiated that requires having attained the age of reason? What is there about Christian initiation that justifies law prohibiting infants from experiencing it fully (canons 891 and 913, §1)? True, infants are not capable of the knowledge and understanding of the age of reason. They cannot have the faith and devotion of 7-year-old children. But do all these required capabilities derive from the meaning of Christian initiation or from the a priori decision to postpone the sacraments of confirmation and first communion according to the former practice and rationale of childhood sacraments?

I rehearse all these questions each time I preside for infant baptism. At the conclusion of that rite, a presider leads god-parents and parents with their babies to the eucharistic table, the symbol of full initiation. There he introduces the Lord's Prayer with words that sound like a ritual apology for incomplete initiation:

> Dearly beloved, these children have been reborn in baptism. Now they are called children of God, for so indeed they are. In confirmation they will receive the fullness of God's Spirit. In holy communion they will share the banquet of Christ's sacrifice, calling God their Father in the midst of the church. (Rite of Baptism for Children, 103)

Is postponement necessary? Why not now?

Incomplete initiation of infants was not the practice and certainly not the norm in early church life. In Rome as late as the thirteenth century, infants as well as adults were fully initiated at Easter. Infants and toddlers shared in communion until the twelfth century, in some places, even later. The RCIA restores celebration of full initiation as the norm. Canon 842, §2 defines full Christian initiation as baptism, confirmation and first communion. Today, except for infants, when the bishop is not presiding at baptism, the presiding presbyter becomes the minister of confirmation so that Christian initiation can be complete rather than partial.

Why this clear preference for full initiation, which challenges our practice of childhood sacraments? In the theological vision of recent liturgical reforms, the sacramental life of the church celebrates the paschal mystery of the Lord experienced in the lives of the faithful. The reform has sought to celebrate this mystery as a unified, integrated and comprehensive reality after centuries of fragmented sacramental life. The annual paschal season was restructured to achieve unity and integration. The Paschal Triduum, which integrates the sufferings-glory, death-resurrection, cross-empty tomb of the Lord, has replaced Easter Sunday alone as our celebration of the Christian pasch. The Christian Sunday was raised up as the premier feast that celebrates the paschal mystery comprehensively conceived.

Complete, as opposed to incomplete, initiation is the norm, because it more holistically proclaims and celebrates the paschal mystery: its unity and integrity. This completeness proclaims the interpersonal relations of the Father, and the Son and the Holy Spirit. And it proclaims the Christian's participation in the dying of the Son, his being raised up by the Father and his transformation into a spirit-filled risen body, a body of spirit-filled disciples by which he is present in the world for the benefit of society. It is the fullness and unity of this mystery that the church celebrates in complete initiation.

When Christian initiation is celebrated completely, there is one presider for all three rites. When baptism is celebrated alone with infants, there are two and sometimes three presiders for the initiation of the same child. When complete initiation is celebrated, the same person is godparent for baptism and confirmation. "This expresses more clearly the relationship between baptism and confirmation" (RC, 5). When baptism is celebrated alone with infants, there are often two different godparents for the initiation of the same child.

To guard against fragmenting the unity of the paschal mystery, the RCIA prescribes the unified or full celebration of initiation. "In accord with the ancient practice of the Roman liturgy, adults are not to be baptized without receiving confirmation immediately afterward, unless some serious reason stands in the way." And the reason for this? "The conjunction of the two celebrations signifies the unity of the paschal mystery, the close link between the mission of the Son and the outpouring of the Holy Spirit, and the connection between the two sacraments through which the Son and the Holy Spirit come with the Father to those who are baptized" (RCIA, 215). Aidan Kavanagh has identified with precision how this rationale challenges our practice of childhood sacraments:

> The theological point made here, RCIA, 215, is of such seriousness that one feels compelled to ask why and how it can be construed as applying only to adults and not to infants and children, especially if they are baptized at the Easter Vigil. Unless the theological point is dismissed as mere rhetoric, it seems inescapable that all who are deemed fit for baptism, no matter what their physical age, should also be confirmed within the same liturgical event. This seems to have in fact been the discipline in the Roman church until the Early Middle Ages, and it is still the practice of the Orthodox churches. The continued Western practice of deferring confirmation of infants and children, more recently even until adolescence, will have to take account of the theological principle stated clearly in RCIA, 215, a principle that would require construal of physical age as "a serious obstacle" to sacramental reception. But if this is proved, then it is inevitable that the same question be posed about baptism of infants: if age is a serious obstacle to receiving confirmation, why then is age not a serious obstacle to receiving baptism? Theological discussion will have to cope with this anomaly. ("Christian Initiation of Adults: The Rites," *Worship* 48 [June-July 1974]: 328)

Deferring confirmation, which is prohibited by RCIA, 215, when baptizing adults, is a major component of our present practice of childhood sacraments. In order to preserve this practice, the exceptive clause of canon 891 has been invoked to allow postponement of confirmation even beyond the age of discretion prescribed in law. However, if the link between baptism and confirmation were to become a more compelling value than teenage confirmation, the same canonical provision could be invoked in the opposite direction: to authorize the confirmation of infants and thus achieve the full and comprehensive celebration of the paschal mystery by full initiation.

Our present practice of baptizing infants without completing their initiation results in an irony. Unbaptized catechumens are graciously welcomed by the church and showered with spiritual benefits (RCIA, 47; canon 206), the greatest of which is full initiation. Members of the faithful—those who have been baptized—enjoy many rights, including the right to the sacraments (canon 213), complete initiation first of all. It is only those infants who come into the church as the newborn of practicing Catholic parents who are denied what is considered for all others a great spiritual benefit and a right: full initiation. Such inhospitality to children and penalty to Catholic parents will not be remedied until we are ready to question our practice of childhood sacraments.

Sacraments of the Church or Sacraments of Individuals

The church celebrates the sacraments of Christian initiation in order to *be* church, as it makes new members. The church seeks to actualize herself by celebrating the paschal mystery as the great reality that is occurring while persons are initiated. Initiation is primarily the proclamation and celebration of the paschal mystery for the sake of the church. We baptize infants without hesitation, because it is the church, first of all, that professes paschal faith. These meanings are embodied and expressed in the structure of the rites, their interrelationship and sequence—baptism, confirmation and first communion—together. In Christian initiation, the church proclaims the meaning of these sacraments.

In our practice of childhood sacraments, on the other hand, the child—the subjective capability of the child and the needs of the child at particular stages of faith development—replaces the church as the principal celebrant and source of the meaning for these sacraments. Sacraments are subjected to the growth needs of children. The meaning that the church proclaims by full initiation is revised to serve strategies of raising a child in the faith. For example, if baptism is not subjectively meaningful to an infant, then confirmation can be used at a later age to achieve that missing meaningfulness. Parents prefer exclusive, family celebrations of infant baptism and "family-style" first communion in which their child is featured with higher profile. In our practice of childhood sacraments, the sacraments of Christian initiation have been uprooted from their context in a journey of faith, psychologized and individualized.

The practice of childhood sacraments and the practice of initiatory sacraments reflect radically different visions of the role of sacramental celebration in the church. As we have seen, the church professes the paschal meaning of these sacraments in full Christian initiation, but a different meaning is expressed in the practice of childhood sacraments.

Sacraments of Initiation or Sacraments of Education

As a result of the subjectivity principle in the practice of childhood sacraments, sacramental preparation of children amounts to religious education: instruction in the faith conducted in classrooms, with textbooks and teachers, as part of the parochial school or religious education curriculum. Before first confession, first communion or confirmation, children are expected to master a certain body of knowledge, in particular to understand the meaning of the particular sacrament they are going to receive next. Admission to the sacrament means successful completion of a level of instruction. The rites and their symbols are analyzed in advance, even rehearsed before they are experienced.

This educational model of sacramental preparation contrasts with catechumenal ministry to unbaptized adults and children. Catechumenal ministry is an all-parish—not a school—ministry. For those of catechetical age, it consists of companioning, storytelling, lectionary-based catechesis, learning to pray and public ritual. Understanding the meaning and reflecting on the symbolism of the sacraments follow a person's experience of them rather than anticipating that experience. Religious education and the academic study of faith are post-initiatory activities. In fact they are founded on the initiatory experience, and their effectiveness depends on it.

The customary sacramental preparation for childhood sacraments stands in marked contrast to the catechumenal ministry described in the RCIA. As a result, unbaptized children and baptized children learn not only different meanings for the same sacraments because they receive them at different times and in a different order; they also experience those sacraments differently because of their broader approach to our life with God, based on experience.

A Possible Pastoral Strategy

Is there any way we can remedy the inconsistency introduced into our parish sacramental practice through the implementation of the RCIA while continuing the practice of "childhood sacraments"? From the previous analysis of these inconsistencies, I believe the following strategy emerges:

When Should the Church Initiate Children? Let us not continue to ask the old questions: "What is the proper age for baptism, for first communion or for confirmation of children?" Instead, ask: "When should the church *initiate* children?" Some children are born into devout Catholic families. Others are already of catechetical age when their parents return to Catholic practice and want them baptized. In any case, the question is: "Should these children be initiated into the church?"

How Can the Three Rites Require Dissimilar Capacities? In answering this question, let us ask another: "What subjective capacity is required of a child in order to become a member of the church?" What is there about the age of reason that makes it a prerequisite for full Christian initiation? What is there about confirmation and first communion that requires the age of discretion? What is there about baptism that makes the age of reason unnecessary? How can the three rites, which together constitute initiation, require dissimilar subjective capacities?

Initiation Should Always Be Full Initiation. Whenever it is time to initiate a person into the church, the initiation should be complete, celebrated fully, with the rites in their proper sequence. If infants are to be baptized, they should be fully initiated like everybody else.

Conclusion

As a corollary, we pastors should more carefully articulate and then address the real needs of Catholic parents in raising their children in the faith. These needs should be addressed today more creatively than by continuing to depend on a misunderstanding of the sacraments of confirmation and eucharist. Because we have become aware of a much larger sacramental tradition, since the prescribed sacramental revision of the Second Vatican Council and since the promulgation of the RCIA, we now recognize these two sacraments—confirmation and eucharist—as sacraments of initiation together with baptism.

The previously described three-point strategy would remove the present sacramental inconsistency. Our parishes would have a consistent practice of Christian initiation, founded on a consistent theology of these sacraments, with consistent catechesis on their meaning—whether we are celebrating them with adults or children, the unbaptized or the baptized.

Meanwhile, as long as our practice of childhood sacraments remains entrenched, unchallenged by the larger tradition, the Second Vatican Council and the RCIA, we will perpetuate two practices of Christian initiation in our parishes, founded on two conflicting theologies of these sacraments, with differing catecheses. And the Grandmother Maes in our parishes, and many others as well, will continue to protest, "But that doesn't make sense, Father!"

Contributors

Kathy Brown—Executive Director, Office for Human Development, Diocese of Phoenix; former director of institutes, North American Forum on the Catechumenate. She has contributed articles to *Breaking Open the Word of God, A Catechumen's Lectionary, Parish Today, Catholic Evangelization, Forum Newsletter* and *Catechumenate: A Journal of Christian Initiation.*

Frank C. Sokol—Presbyter of the diocese of Pittsburgh, diocesan director for religious education/CCD. He has written articles on issues related to the catechumenate for *Christian Initiation Resources, Pastoral Music, Catechist, Forum Newsletter, Living Light* and *Catechumenate: A Journal of Christian Initiation.*

215

Mary Collins, OSB—Professor of pastoral liturgy at the Catholic University of America. Her recent publications include *Women at Prayer, Worship: Renewal to Practice, The Fate of Confession, Women: Invisible Church and Society.* She is coeditor of and contributor to the *New Dictionary of Theology.*

Catherine Dooley, OP—Professor of catechetics and sacraments in the department of religion and religious education at the Catholic University of America. Her religious education writings include *The Jesus Book, The Mary Book, The Saints Book* and *The Gift of Peace.* Her liturgical writings have appeared in *New Catholic World, Catechumenate: A Journal of Christian Initiation* and *Living Light.*

Robert D. Duggan—Pastor of St. Rose of Lima Parish, Gaithersburg, Maryland. He authored "Conversion in the *Ordo initiationis Christianae adultorum,*" in *Ephemerides Liturgicae*; "Reaction from an RCIA Perspective," in *Alternative Futures for Worship: Baptism and Confirmation.* He edited *Conversion and the Catechumenate.*

Linda L. Gaupin, CDP—Director of the Office for Worship for the diocese of Wilmington. She completed her doctoral work on sacramental catechesis at the Catholic University of America and is on the graduate faculty of LaSalle University, Philadelphia. She has written numerous articles on liturgical and sacramental catechesis in scholarly, pastoral and popular collections and journals.

Grace Harding—Director of special educational programs for the diocese of Pittsburgh. She has written a column in *Catechist* for several years.

Aidan Kavanagh, OSB—Monk of the Archabbey of St. Meinrad and professor of liturgics at the Divinity School, Yale University. He authored *The Shape of Baptism: The Rite of Christian Initiation, Confirmation: Origins and Reform* and many other books and articles on public worship.

Berard L. Marthaler, OFM CONV—Professor of catechetics in the department of religion and religious education at the Catholic University of America. He is editor of the *Living Light* and author of *The Creed.*

Richard P. Moudry—Pastor, Church of Christ the King, Minneapolis, Minnesota. He authored "The Initiation of Children: The Path One Parish Took" in *Catechumenate: A Journal of Christian Initiation* (July 1987).

Don Neumann—Pastor of St. Pius V Church, Pasadena, Texas, chairperson of the RCIA committee for the diocese of Houston, member of the steering committee for the North American Forum on the Catechumenate.

Richelle Pearl-Koller—Pastoral associate, Church of Christ the King, Minneapolis, Minnesota; wife, mother, educator. She serves on the steering committee of the North American Forum on the Catechumenate.

Paul J. Philibert, OP—Provincial prior of the Southern Dominican Province, New Orleans. He is a specialist in Christian ethics and the formation of conscience.

John H. Westerhoff III—Professor of religion and education at Duke University Divinity School. He is the author of many books, including *Inner Growth/Outer Change: An Educational Guide to Church Renewal, Will Our Children Have Faith? Building God's People in a Materialistic Society, Living the Faith Community: The Church That Makes a Difference,* and *A Pilgrim People: Learning through the Church Year.*

For Further Reading

Bernardin, Joseph. *Access to the Sacraments of Initiation and Reconciliation for Developmentally Disabled Persons* (Chicago: Liturgy Training Publications, 1985).

Brusselmans, Christiane. "From RCIC to RCIA and Back to RCIC: The Christian Initiation of Children," in *Forum Newsletter* (Fall 1986), 1–4.

Catechumenate: A Journal of Christian Initiation (March 1989), Proceedings of the Consultation on the Catechumenate for Children of Catechetical Age, December 4–7, 1988, sponsored by the North American Forum on the Catechumenate.

Duggan, Robert D., ed. *Conversion and the Catechumenate* (New York: Paulist Press, 1984).

Dunning, James B. *New Wine, New Wine Skins* (New York: William H. Sadlier, 1981).

Kavanagh, Aidan. *Confirmation: Origins and Reform* (New York: Pueblo Publishing Company, 1987).

_____. *The Shape of Baptism: The Rite of Christian Initiation* (New York: Pueblo Publishing Company, 1974).

Lewinski, Ron. *Guide for Sponsors* Revised Edition (Chicago: Liturgy Training Publications, 1987).

Marthaler, Berard L. *The Creed* (Mystic, Connecticut: Twenty-Third Publications, 1987).

Osborne, Kenan. *The Christian Sacraments of Initiation* (New York: Paulist Press, 1987).

Rite of Christian Initiation of Adults: Complete Text of the Rite Together with Additional Rites Approved for Use in the Dioceses of the United States of America, prepared by the International Commission on English in the Liturgy and Bishops' Commission on the Liturgy of the National Conference of Catholic Bishops (Chicago: Liturgy Training Publications, 1988).

Searle, Mark, ed. *Alternative Futures for Worship: Baptism and Confirmation* (Collegeville: The Liturgical Press, 1987).

Turner, Paul. *The Meaning and Practice of Confirmation* (New York: Peter Lang, Inc., 1987).

Westerhoff, John H., III. *A Pilgrim People: Learning through the Church Year* (New York: Harper and Row, 1984).

Wilde, James A., ed. *Before and after Baptism: The Work of Teachers and Catechists* (Chicago: Liturgy Training Publications, 1988).

_____, ed. *When Should We Confirm: The Order of Initiation* (Chicago: Liturgy Training Publications, 1989).